Play Piano in a Flash!

Visit the author at:

www.scottthepianoguy.com

Play Piano in a Flash!

Scott Houston

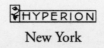

New York

B&N Edition ISBN: 1-4013-2224-7
        ISBN-13: 978-1-4013-2224-3

This edition specially produced for Barnes & Noble by Hyperion.

To my beautiful baby girl McKenna,
& her beautiful mother, Theresa.

Thanks for all the Joy!

Contents

Chapter 5
Learning Chords - Pain or Pleasure?..........37

Chapter 6
Let's Get Down to Business and Start Playing..........43

Chapter 7
**How to Lose All Respect for Piano Players
in One Easy Chapter**..........53

FOREWORD

I would like to give credit to a few people who have had a big impact on my piano playing life. In three different ways these people pushed me closer and closer to my current role as a zealot out there convincing people that yes, they can play piano – and better yet, actually have fun while learning to play it!

First, thanks to the late John Radd. John was a great jazz player whom I came across at a music camp I attended when I was a kid. At the time I was playing the heck out of a drumset. I had actually reached a fairly high level of accomplishment through high school and had been accepted into a very prestigious university music program. Over a summer break, I attended a monthlong jazz camp in Shell Lake, Wisconsin. They were starting the drummers at a very beginning level, and I didn't want to waste my time in there for the first week. Instead, I thought I'd go sit in on the piano group. I had taken some lessons when I was a kid, but never considered myself a "player" in any way. Piano was just a good tool I needed to know something about as a sideline to my (in my dreams) future career as a famous drummer in a famous band.

In the course of about a day and a half, I had my whole musical life yanked out from under me. John laid out for a bunch of us wet-behind-the-ears kids the basics of what I will lay out for you in this book. I sat there for the entire day with my jaw hanging wide open thinking, "You mean this is all there is to it? You mean that's how you guys sound so hip all the time?" Well, in hindsight, it was one of those real life-changing moments. John swung open a giant barn door that I have yet to quit walking through. What it amounted to was that for the first time, I realized I could play piano the way I wanted to without the agonizing thought of years and years of traditional classical piano lessons. Although I was far from having it "under hand" at the time, I could absolutely see the light at the end of the tunnel. The best part was that it was right in front of me. Not multiple years down the road of arduous and non-fun lessons. And I could have fun playing tunes I wanted to play – the way I wanted to play them. From that day on, I played more and more piano, and less and less drums. Bless John Radd's heart, he let out "the secret" that I have been screaming from the mountaintop in workshops ever since. Don't worry, you'll know it too after you read this book.

Next I want to thank Norm Mazurowski, at that time the general manager of the private country club near where I grew up. You see, after the aforementioned epiphany that I had at the camp, I now felt the overwhelming confidence (however misplaced) that I was a "real" piano player. All of a sudden, I could sound like the pros, so why not go out and work real gigs like the pros?

I marched down to the club and offered my services to play cocktail piano for their dinner patrons a few nights a week. Norm (amazingly) agreed and we proceeded to work out a deal for me to play there for three hours a few nights a week for a few months.

It was only during my first night, at my first piano gig ever, that I came to the shocking realization that the sum total of my repertoire (that being four or five tunes) would last me about fifteen minutes – yet I still had over two hours to go. Although I looked ever so continental in my tux, I was near a total and complete anxiety attack right there in the country club. So needless to say, my breaks were a little (OK, a whole lot) longer than they should have been. Also, I kept an eagle eye on when new people would be seated for dinner near the piano. As soon as that happened, I would launch back into my tried and true five songs for another "go 'round."

I just kept hoping that the wait staff, and especially Norm, were so busy doing their jobs that they wouldn't notice that I had disguised playing the famous Latin standard "Girl from Ipanema" eight times that night by using different tempos and styles, whether it really worked or not. Believe me, an uptempo swinging version of "Ipanema" is not a good thing for recently ingested country club food. (Now that I'm recalling it, I keep hearing that bouncy theme from "I Dream of Jeannie"....Oooh... scary...)

Anyway, Norm was nice enough to stick with me for a few months. Believe me, I knew A LOT more tunes when I finished that gig than when I started. So thanks, Norm. I attribute my first burst of learning a few tunes to you (even though I still get nauseous thinking about that night).

It also was my first experience, although I didn't realize it at the time, discovering that my playing was getting better and better through *playing* and learning new tunes, not practicing. More on that in the book.

Finally, I must mention my most recent influence and, dare I say, mentor, Robert Laughlin. I use the term mentor not in a typical way. It is not his playing or teaching that have been such a positive influence (although he does both quite well). What Robert has done (and continues to do with his very successful publishing business, The New School of American Music) is put down in black and white what all of us players have been doing for years.

It is not that what he espouses is new and unique; anyone who has ever played cocktail (or pop style) piano uses the techniques he teaches. It is just that in the past the only way to get the information was through word of mouth, or at esoteric things like the jazz camp I attended years ago.

It was as though you needed to be "in the secret club" to get this information from other musicians. The only problem was that no one knew what the "club" was called or when it met.

Robert solidified my feelings that there is no crime in bringing this information to everyone. Whether or not you are going to "pay your dues" and loyally live a life of financial hardship as a starving musician shouldn't affect your ability to find out how to have fun playing the piano.

There are professional musicians, and then there are the other 99.9% of the population. It's that 99.9% that Robert has helped convince me deserve a chance to play piano for one reason – to have fun. No more, no less – just for enjoyment.

Read on and I'll tell you how…

INTRODUCTION

THE "CLASSICAL CONUNDRUM"

OK, so that I don't have any rioting piano teachers show-ing up at my doorstep, I want to make one thing perfectly clear right at the start:

THIS BOOK WILL ABSOLUTELY POSITIVELY NOT TEACH YOU HOW TO PLAY CLASSICAL PIANO.

There, I said it.

However, in the interest of fairness I would like to make another statement:

USING THE RULES AND TECHNIQUES OF CLASSICAL PIANO IS TOTALLY WRONG AND INAPPROPRIATE FOR PLAYING NON-CLASSICAL MUSIC.

Sounds pretty strange, huh? Well, it is so important that it bears a little more discussion. Just as musically immoral as it would be for me to state that the rules and techniques used to play a non-classical style of piano would be OK to use when playing a classical piece of music, it is equally true of the inverse. That is, to try and play non-classical music using the rules the vast majority of us learned in typical piano lessons is equally as wrong and musically immoral. Yet that is what happens all the time because the overwhelming majority of us were taught classical piano techniques by our private teachers. However, if you try to play non-classical piano using those techniques, you are doing it wrong. It is simply stylistically incorrect to play either style using the rules and techniques of the other.

Now I am painting a pretty broad stroke here, and I acknowledge that maybe a few of you learned to play some piano on your own, or that maybe even fewer of you actually learned to play pop style (i.e. non-classical) piano from a teacher. But from my experience with the overwhelming number of teachers I have spoken to, and the overwhelming number of attendees of my workshops, you are a statistical needle in a haystack if you received anything other than traditional classical piano instruction when you took lessons.

Let me make this next point loud and clear as well. It is not as though a teacher is trying to do anyone a disservice by teaching the way they do. I am in no way suggesting there is some master evil plot being acted out by the thousands of traditional piano teachers out there. Quite to the contrary, the vast majority of teachers with whom I've ever been associated are extremely dedicated and responsible. It is simply a case of them, one, teaching the way they were taught (and in many cases with the same materials), and two, not knowing how to play any style other than classical. It is a strange truism that not many piano teachers are out working gigs for a living, and not many pianists out working for a living teach piano. They tend to be two totally different animals that don't hang out much together.

Now here is some possibly bad, but true, news. If you *do* want to learn how to play classical piano well, I don't know any other way than to start taking lessons once a week for the next five to ten years (OK, maybe I am exaggerating, and it really should be only three to five years). The road to "classi-calville" is a long and arduous one.

Here is some good, and equally true, news. If you want to learn how to play non-classical popular style piano, you simply need to learn a basic set of rules and techniques and you can start sounding fairly hip right away (as in hours or days, not years). Will you want to keep learning and playing and otherwise keep getting better for the next five to ten years? YES! But, you'll be having the time of your life on the way there. Why? Because you'll be *playing* instead of *practicing*.

Now I'm sure you're saying to yourself, "Sounds great, Scott, but how can it be that easy to teach?" Well, the reason playing non-classical piano is so much easier to teach someone is that it removes the "A-Number-1 Top-of-the-List" reason that most people never learn to play classical piano at any level of proficiency. That, my friends, is notation reading.

You know, getting your hands around a piano is a relatively simple thing to do compared to most other instruments. It's all target practice! Seriously, as long as you get your finger over the right note at the right time, you are good to go. You can't control if the piano is in or out of tune. You don't have to worry about taking a deep enough breath. Pianists don't have to get their mouths in some correctly contorted position (known as an embouchure) like horn players. Think about poor brass players whose lips get all swollen and puffy and hurt when they play high notes. Or how about oboe players who must be (at least I know I would be) concerned about their brains squeezing out their ears when they play. Or how about any of you who have had sons or daughters start out on a reed instrument like a clarinet or saxophone. I mean, a better goose call has yet to be invented than the first week of a reed player's musical life.

In exchange for the extremely difficult task of dealing with a tough instrument, everyone else gets totally bailed out when it comes to note reading. With just a few exceptions (like string players every now and then) all they ever have to read is one note at a time and only in one clef! Must be nice! Think about traditional piano music: multiple notes at one time, in two clefs (which are different), with two hands. It's a brain buster for sure!

The thing that makes playing piano such a killer is not the *playing*, it's the *note reading*. Piano players (or wannabe players) are strange in this way; I bet if I had 100 piano students look at traditional sheet music (that I knew had notation in it tougher than they could read), 95% of them would say "Scott, I can't play that." What they should have said is "Scott, I can't *read* that." Those students wouldn't have any idea whether or not they could physically get their hands over the keyboards in such a way as to play what that notation was recording. I'm sure they never got remotely close to testing their physical abilities on a keyboard. That is because they (like the overwhelming majority of failed "lesson takers") never got to be good enough notation readers to even come close to testing their mechanical abilities.

It may seem like a hair-splitting distinction, but it is really a huge issue that you must come to grips with: READING NOTATION DOES NOT EQUAL GOOD PIANO PLAYING. Can both coincide (good reading and good playing)? Sure, and I applaud those who have toiled to a position where that is the case! But two other possibilities are found in abundance as well: one being great notation readers who can't play their way out of a paper bag; the other being those that can't read worth a hoot who are GREAT players.

It is that last description that is of major intrigue to us in this book. I hope you are all quietly thinking to yourself, "You mean I can learn how to play piano without becoming a great note reader?" The answer is a resounding YES!!! We will have to acquire a *very* basic amount of notation reading skill. But the extremely difficult task of honing your note reading skills that classical students are required to endure for years and years is *totally nonexistent* as a requirement for playing non-classical piano.

In summary, I reiterate that what you will learn in this book is NOT appropriate for use in playing classical-style piano. But, always keep in mind the other side of the coin. If you use the rules of classical piano to play non-classical music, you too will be playing incorrectly. Worse yet, you will be doomed to sound like a corny sheet music player, not like a pro. I'll show you how to sound like a pro...

CHAPTER 2

HELP, I CAN'T READ MUSIC!

Remember, I said we are going to have to learn a very minimal amount of note reading to play music in this style correctly. That is what we'll deal with in this section.

Those of you who have had any musical training at all, be it piano or some other instrument, will probably be able to skip this section. At the most, maybe you should skim over it to refresh your memory. But I'm sure you will find this completely <u>un</u>threatening from a mental challenge standpoint. All the rest of you, try to act brave and read on...

SOME GOOD NEWS & SOME BAD NEWS

I have some terrible news for all of you reading this book. As my wife's obstetrician once said before the birth of our child, "better to just come out with it." OK, here goes...

You must learn how to read a one-note-at-a-time sequence of notes in the treble clef.

Now, I have some great news for all of you reading this book. OK, here goes again...

You must learn how to read a one-note-at-a-time sequence of notes in the treble clef.

Sound familiar? It's one of those good news, bad news things. Here is the scoop:

To play the style of notation that we need to learn to sound like a pro, we need to get to a point where we can read a melody line (a fancy name for a consecutive string of notes) that will be notated in the treble clef. The fantastic thing about this is that once we get there, we're done (from a note-reading standpoint)!

Here are a few very salient points to ward off any impending panic attacks from you total non-readers out there.

- The melody line will only be one note at a time. Never multiple notes at once.
- It will *always* be in the treble clef. Now you won't have to read two different clefs at once. If you don't even know what a clef is yet, don't panic. Just take my increasingly believable word for it that this is GREAT news. For those of you who *do* realize how good this news is… one, two, three… YIPPEEE!!!!
- For the final "maybe I *can* do this" kick in the pants, I want you to know that when they start kids in band, everyone in the room is reading a one note melody line in the treble clef by Thursday or Friday of the very first week. *(Except for drummers, who are a totally different branch in the band evolutionary chart. In fact, most drummers I've known are a totally different branch of the human evolutionary chart as well. I'm allowed to say this. I was a drummer in band.)* Believe me, if all of those rugrats can do it, so can you!

OK, let's dig in and learn what we need to know about music notation…

THE "KEY-NOTE" SPEECH

First, let's look at a keyboard. No matter what the total number of keys you have on your keyboard (a full size piano has 88) all keyboards are made up of 12 white and black keys that repeat over and over. They look like this…

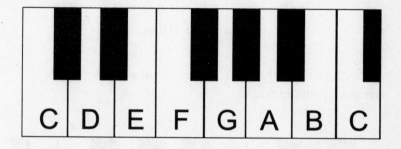

Notice that the black keys come in sets of twos and threes. You can find a "C" note on a piano quickly because it is the white key directly to the left of a set of two black keys. Middle C is the C closest to the middle of your keyboard. Clever the way they came up with that name, huh?

Now, let's figure out the names of the black keys. Notice that you can describe the same black key by saying it is either up (to the right) from its nearest white key or down (to the left) from its nearest white key. Because it can be described both ways, each black key has two names. It is exactly the same key. It can simply be called by two different names.

If you are describing it as being up from a white key you call it a "sharp" of the white key, such as "C-sharp." If instead you want to describe it as being down from the white key, you call it a "flat" of the white key, such as "D-flat." Remember, sharps go up and flats go down.

Finally, the symbols used to denote sharps and flats look like this:

$$\sharp \text{ (sharp), or } \flat \text{ (flat)}$$

So, here is another look at a keyboard with the names of the black notes included:

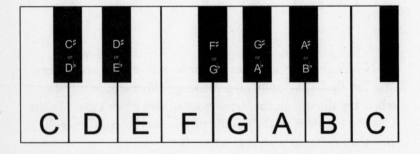

Now we need to figure out the correlation between the names of the notes themselves and how they are represented in music notation.

NO BASS CLEF EVER AGAIN!

When you look at most sheet music you will see two symbols at the beginning of two sets of five lines:

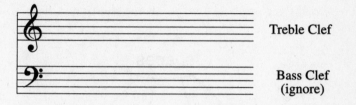

Treble Clef

Bass Clef
(ignore)

The set of five lines on top (with the thing that looks like a curvy "S") is called the treble clef and is the only one you will be interested in for our style of piano. Classical players use both of them, but you will NEVER have to read the lower one (called the bass clef). You can totally ignore it!

DOES "EVERY GOOD BOY DOES FINE" OR "FACE" SOUND FAMILIAR?

Looking at only the treble clef, each of the five lines represents a different key on the piano, and each of the four spaces between the lines also represents a different key. The five lines, from the bottom to the top, represent E,G,B,D, and F. That is what "Every Good Boy Does Fine" refers to. As a memory aid, if you take the first letter of each of those words in order, you will end up with E,G,B,D, and F. The spaces between the lines (again from the bottom to the top) represent F,A,C, and E. If you go sequentially up every line and space, you will find that they represent the keys one after another on a keyboard.

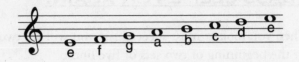

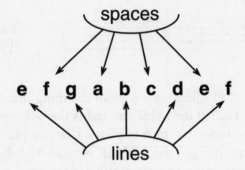

The line or space that a note head (the little solid or hollow ovals you see all over music) is sitting on tells you what key on the piano to play.

Oh, and by the way, you read music just like a book, from left to right, top to bottom.

No, ledger lines are not only for accountants

If a note is above or below the five lines, you need to keep counting step-wise every other line and space up or down the keyboard until you get to the note in question. As you move farther away from the five lines that make up the staff, you keep adding these little lines as needed to keep the "line-space-line-space" routine going. Those little "mini" lines (or dashes) are called ledger lines in music parlance. Again, just remember that every line or space sequentially represents another key up or down on a keyboard.

How not to have sharp and flat anxiety

If a ♯ (sharp) or ♭ (flat) is sitting on a line or space at the beginning of the line of music, that means you must play ANY note that occurs on that line or space, all the way through the music, as a sharp or flat depending on what symbol is shown. For example, if there is a ♭ (flat) symbol sitting on the third line (the "b" line) at the beginning of the staff, like this:

Then you must play any B that you come across in the entire piece of music as a B♭. Also (although this seems pretty obvious), if you come across just a single notehead with a ♯ (sharp) or ♭ (flat) in front of it, as opposed to the symbol being at the beginning of a staff, you just play that single note as it is denoted, sharped or flatted. *(Technically, you would also play any other of the same note within that single measure, although it is seldom notated that way these days.)*

In essence, if the sharp or flat symbol is at the beginning of a staff, it affects all of the notes throughout the piece. If it is elsewhere in the music, it just affects the note to which it is directly attached.

WHY YOU SHOULD NEVER PLAY RHYTHMS AS NOTATED

You know what key to play based on what line or space the note is sitting on. Now we'll look at how long to hold it down. Keep in mind that unlike classical music, in which it is vital to play rhythms exactly as written, in non-classical playing it is actually *incorrect* to play things exactly as written. Music in this style is meant only as a guide, from which you can stray a bit to interpret it as you desire. So do not get hung up trying to "count" perfectly as do so many "ex" piano students. Try to play the rhythms as you would whistle or hum them if you were leisurely walking down the street.

Having said that, on this page you will find the guidelines for what notes look like and their duration relative to each other:

NOTE DURATIONS

𝐨 = Whole Note – 4 beats

♩ = Half Note – 2 beats

♩ = Quarter Note – 1 beat

♪ = Eighth Note – 2 of them equal 1 beat.
They can also be connected like this:

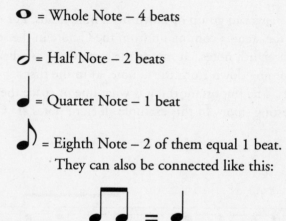

♪ = Sixteenth Note – 4 of them equal 1 beat.

They can also be connected like this:

If you ever see a dot after a note, just increase its duration by half of its original value. For example, if a half note equals 2 beats, a dotted half note equals 3.

♩. = 3 beats

Also, stems can go up or down from note heads. For example, here the stem is coming up from the C note in the second set of four eighth notes. It means the same thing as when the stem is coming down from the C note, as in the first set of four notes. The important thing is what line or space the note head is resting upon. In this example all eight notes are C's.

Finally, when we refer to beats, many find it simpler to think of beats in terms of tapping your foot. For example, a half note is two foot taps while a quarter note is only one. The important thing is to keep the tapping steady and consistent so that all the different note durations stay in the correct proportion to one another.

ONE NOTE AT A TIME

Now take a look at the following familiar melodies. Take advantage of the fact that you probably already know what these simple tunes sound like. Now connect what you just learned about notation with what you know these songs should sound like. Try to play these simple melodies on your keyboard with your right hand.

Don't worry about what fingers to use. Just do what feels most natural to you. The bigger objective is to quickly identify what keys to play, and how long to play them, based on the notes you are reading.

SOME SIMPLE MELODIES

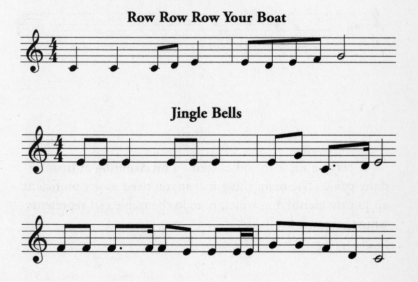

Row Row Row Your Boat

Jingle Bells

My Country 'Tis of Thee

Joy to the World

If playing these melodies seems a bit daunting at first, don't panic. The main thing is that you need to get proficient at quickly identifying which note in the treble clef represents which key on a keyboard.

CHORD SYMBOLS & WHY WE LOVE THEM SO MUCH

You might have asked yourself after hearing me state that all we are going to ever need to read is a one note melody line, "Well where are we going to come up with all of the rest of the notes? I've never seen a cocktail lounge piano player playing just one note at a time!"

Point well taken. Now we have to find a way to figure out what other notes to hit to play a song correctly. But I also hemmed myself in by stating that we wouldn't have to read more notation than the one note at a time. What gives? Chord symbols, that's what.

Chord symbols are a way to tell a piano player what other notes to play without forcing them to read music notation. It is kind of like musical stenography because one symbol represents many notes.

You are going to find that chord symbols are like the secret treasure map to finding the riches of playing non-classical piano. What's more, by using chord symbols for your playing, you'll be using the technique that pros have used for years!

So let's get into these chord symbol things in a little bit more detail...

WHERE DO YOU FIND CHORD SYMBOLS?

Chord symbols are found in probably 95% of non-classical sheet music ever printed. As I have given workshops around the country over the years, it has amazed me how few piano players ever even knew chord symbols were in music, let alone how to read them. One big reason chord symbols are almost always included in sheet music is for guitar players. Well, we need to take a page out of the guitar players' repertoire and learn how to read chord symbols. Guitar players have always had it easy. They all were taught about chord symbols from day one. Poor piano players on the other hand may never be taught about chord symbols, or if they're lucky they might get exposed to chord symbols after suffering through several years of formal lessons. You, my friends, are not going to have that problem. Let's find out right now how to read chord symbols. You soon will be able to consider yourself "in the know."

Chord symbols are always shown in notation above the treble clef. They look like capital letters, sometimes with sharps or flats or numbers and other things after them. See them in the example snippet below:

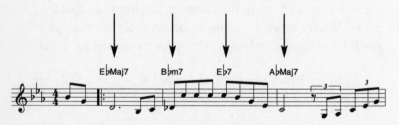

The task at hand is to figure out what chord you need to be playing based on what the chord symbol is above the melody line. So let's start at the very beginning.

WHAT IS A CHORD?

A chord is simply two or more notes played at the same time. Nothing technical about it. Play a C, C#, and D note down together at the same time. Yuch! Sounds terrible, but it's a chord. Now play C-E-G-B all at the same time. Ahh... much better. It too is a chord. Usually, in our type of playing, the chords you use will have three or four notes in them. But by definition, they could have more or less.

THE YIN & YANG OF A CHORD SYMBOL— ROOT & FLAVOR

You can always split a chord symbol into two parts: the root and what I like to call the "flavor" (OK you serious pianists, I know that isn't the technical term, but phooey on youey, it's my book and I'm sticking with flavor.) The root is simply the letter name at the beginning of the symbol (including the sharp or flat, if there is one). Sometimes, the root is all the symbol has, which by default means the flavor is major. (I'll explain further in a few more sentences.)

So for example:

Chord Symbol	Root	"Flavor"
C	C	Major
A7	A	Seventh
Fmin	F	Minor
C#7	C#	Seventh

Now the reason the root is called the root is because it "anchors" the chord. In its simplest form the root is the first, or lowest, note of the chord. For example, a C chord starts with a C note, an F7 chord starts with an F note, and a Gmin chord starts with a G chord. Pretty much rocket science, isn't it?

In chord symbol notation, if there is ever just a root with nothing after it, by default it means the flavor is Major. (Don't worry if you don't know what Major means yet—we're just trying to figure out how to read the dang things.) Major is like the default booby-prize chord flavor in that if a chord symbol doesn't tell you anything else after the root, you're supposed to know that it signifies a major flavor.

Another good thing about knowing the root is that it is probably the most important note in the chord. Unless you have the luxury of playing with a bass player (whose primary directive in his/her musical life is to play the roots, by the way), you will always need to get the root played somehow. So, lucky for you, the instant you see a chord symbol, BANG, you know the root. It is just the letter name at the beginning of the symbol. Onward to the flavors...

There are many different flavors a chord can take, but chords can all be distilled into seven major categories: Major, minor, seventh, Major seventh, minor seventh, augmented, and diminished. Here is what they look like in chord symbol notation (all assuming a root of C).

Chord Symbol	Root	"Flavor"
C	C	Major
Cmin	C	minor
C7	C	seventh
Cmaj7	C	Major seventh
Cmin7	C	minor seventh
Caug	C	augmented
Cdim	C	diminished

In the interest of full disclosure, there are a couple of other ways that you might see these chords notated. There aren't chord symbol "police" that keep a rigid standard. People notate them a little differently. Sometimes for a minor chord you will see a single lowercase "m" instead of "min." Sometimes for a Major seventh you will see just an upper case "M7" instead of "maj7." Also, in some cases you may see an augmented chord notated with a single "+" instead of "aug," and you might see a diminished chord shown as a little circle (like a degree or Fahrenheit sign) instead of "dim" (C+ or C° for augmented and diminished, respectively).

There are more chord flavors than these six basic types; however all others just build on them, which makes their chord symbols obvious. For example Cmin9 is undoubtedly a "C minor 9th" chord. It is beyond the scope of this book to get into every possible chord you may ever run across. Suffice it to say that by knowing how to read these seven symbols, you'll be in good shape for getting your piano playing well on its way.

In summary, you need to get to a point where you can quickly identify what a chord type is by looking at its symbol. Luckily it's easy to figure out this chord symbol notation. They aren't in some top secret code, for Pete's sake! For example, how much memory skill does it take to remember that "aug" means augmented and that "min" means minor? Thank goodness, not much (or I wouldn't have ever been able to do it...).

CHAPTER 4

THE MAKINGS OF A CHORD

Well folks, we've finally gotten to the crux of the matter at hand. Now we need to explore what, in fact, makes a Major a Major, and a minor a minor, and so on. However, before I launch into a "major" assault (pardon the pun) on all of this, I want to offer you an "out" so to speak.

Major Disclaimer #1

I am terribly concerned that some of you will look at this next section, get a glazed look in your eyes and start muttering something about "same ole' piano lessons…" and walk away from what is close to becoming the chance to knock a lifelong dream off your list of to-do's. I feel the need to include this next section on explaining chords more as a "reference" for you to use should you need it, than as a suggestion as to how to learn all of your chords. If for any reason you feel the need to skip over this section – knock yourself out. You won't offend me a bit. Just know that should you need this information down the road, it will be here.

IT'S ALL ABOUT HALF STEPS, MY DEAR

All right, let's make some sense of this major minor hub-bub... Let's talk about a keyboard for a minute. I'm not thinking notation here, I'm talking about a real keyboard out in the real world. The closest distance between two keys on a keyboard is called a "half step." What I mean by that is that you can't get to any key between the two in question. As long as that is the case, then the distance between the two is a half step. For example if you go from a C to a D on a piano, is that a half step? No, because between those two keys is another key, the black one in between them (C#). Now if you go from a C to a C# is that a half-step? Yes. Because they are the closest two keys to each other without another one in between them. They are a half step apart.

So, what is a half step higher than an A? An A#. What is a half step higher than an F#? A G.

OK, then what is a half step higher than an E? An F. Whoa there... take a look at that one. Every other time a half step has been going from a white to a black key, or a black to a white key. But in this case it was from white to white? Yup, that's right. The rule is that they need to be the closest keys to each other to be a half step apart. Because of the two odd-ball places on a piano between a B and a C, and between an E and an F where there is no black note, the distances between those two notes is only a half step. Just remember, closest two keys together equals a half step.

Now for this next one you get three chances, and the first two don't count. Guess what you call two half steps put together? Class...class? Correctamundo! A whole step. Just as logical as it sounds, two half steps equal one whole step. For example if C to C# is one half step, and C# to D is the next half step, then C up to D is a whole step.

Why do I submit you to such mental torture as having to figure out half and whole steps? Because that is how I am going to describe to you the different chord structures that make a Major a Major and a minor a minor, and so on.

THE TWO VARIABLES OF A CHORD FLAVOR

You can build a chord by describing the distance (in half steps) between the notes. It's kind of like one of those trip routers you can get for vacations. You remember, "Start here, go so many miles, turn left, go so many miles, etc." until you get to your destination. Well, for learning chords we're going to say "Start here, go so many half steps, then go on so many more half steps, etc." until you have all of the notes in the chord figured out. The note you start on will always be the root.

Let me show you how this works… A C chord (remember that is a Major flavor, because there was nothing after the root in the chord symbol) has three notes in it: C, E, and G.

I could also describe a C chord to you by saying this: "Start by playing a C, then go up four half steps and play that note, then go up an additional three half steps and play that note." If you did that, you would be playing C, E, and G.

1) *Start on the root, which is C*
2) *Go up 4 half-steps to E*
3) *Go up 3 more half-steps to G*

So, what makes a particular chord flavor a unique chord flavor are two things: 1. the number of notes in the chord (in this case three) and 2. the distance between those notes (in this case, root, up four half steps, then up three half steps).

Once you know those two variables, you can build that particular flavor starting on any root. It's kind of like having a universal translator that will let you build that chord no matter on which note you start. Let's try it out.

Again we said that our two variables for a Major chord are:

- three notes
- the distance between them is root, up four half steps, up three half steps.

Knowing that, let's figure out what notes are in an F (Major) chord:

Start on F (the root), go up four half steps to A, then go up three more half steps to C.

That's it! An F chord is F, A, C.

Son of a gun, it works!

1) Start on the root, which is F
2) Go up 4 half-steps to A
3) Go up 3 more half-steps to C

Let's try it one more time just to practice. This time let's figure out a D chord:

Start on D (the root), go up four half steps to F#, then go up three more half steps to A.

Bingo! A "D" chord is D, F#, A.

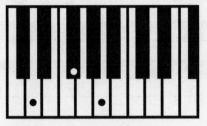

1) Start on the root, which is D
2) Go up 4 half-steps to F#
3) Go up 3 more half-steps to A

OK, now that you know that we can describe any chord by telling two pieces of information, I can go ahead and give you a chart that will tell you the other chord flavors on the next page.

Chord flavor	Number of notes	Distance between notes (in half steps, R=root)	Example using C as the root
Major	3	R-4-3	C C-E-G
minor	3	R-3-4	Cmin C-E♭-G
seventh	4	R-4-3-3	C7 C-E-G-B♭
Major seventh	4	R-4-3-4	Cmaj7 C-E-G-B
minor seventh	4	R-3-4-3	Cmin7 C-E♭-G-B♭
augmented	3	R-4-4	Caug C-E-G-♯
diminished	3	R-3-3	Cdim C-E♭-G♭

Just to run through a couple more of these as examples, let's figure out a G7 chord.

Start on G, go up four half steps to B, go up three half steps to D, go up three half steps to F.

G7 = G, B, D, F

1) Start on the root, which is G
2) Go up 4 half-steps to B
3) Go up 3 more half-steps to D
4) Go up 3 more half-steps to F

How about an "Adim" chord?

Start on A, go up three half steps to C, go up three half steps to Eb

Adim = A, C, Eb

1) Start on the root, which is A
2) Go up 3 half-steps to C
3) Go up 3 more half-steps to Eb

Finally, an Emaj7 chord.

Start on E, go up four half steps to G#, go up three half steps to B, go up four half steps to D#.

Emaj7 = E, G#, B, D#

1) Start on the root, which is E
2) Go up 4 half-steps to G#
3) Go up 3 more half-steps to B
4) Go up 4 more half-steps to D#

So there you have it! Now you know what makes a particular chord flavor what it is. As you play through some of these, you will very quickly start to recognize what the different flavors sound like. Remember, the only difference between chords of the same flavor is what note you start it on (the root).

CHAPTER 5

LEARNING CHORDS—
PAIN OR PLEASURE?

At this juncture you are probably asking yourself, "How should I go about learning some chords, now that I know what makes them tick?"

Here comes one of those comments that at first blush will probably sound so obvious that you'll think "of course," but unfortunately almost no one takes its heed.

*"If you're going to have to learn a few chords,
why not learn the chords to the tune you've
always wanted to play the most, first?"*

Seriously, it is not like any one chord is more difficult than another – they are all just different. On piano, unlike almost all other instruments, it is really an exercise of "target practice." That is, you just need to worry about getting your fingers over the right notes. But the point is that the notes are equally easy to play. It isn't the case that an F chord, for example, is tougher to play than any other chord, it is simply different. Almost all other instruments have it a *lot* tougher. Either notes get harder as you get higher or lower (like a high note on a trumpet for example), or some notes or chords are simply harder based on hand position (ask a guitar player how long it took her to play her first F chord). Well, on a piano, all notes and chords are equal from an ease-of-playing standpoint. Once you press down the key, your work is done! You can't control whether the piano is in or out of tune, or what it sounds like.

Everyone else has to spend a lot of effort on things like intonation, breath control, and position of the mouth (for wind instruments, obviously). Not us, we've got it easy. It's just target practice.

If that is the case, then why do so many people go down this excruciatingly slow and, most of all, BORING, path of starting out with one chord type (usually major, mistakenly thinking it is the easiest) learning it up, down, inside, out, and every which way in between? Then they go to the next chord type (usually minor), doing the same thing, and on and on and on … In the process probably 99% of prospective pianists bail out because of one big issue: They never get to play anything that sounds remotely good. They are too busy *practicing* to ever get to the *playing!* Get the point?

TWO ROUTES TO THE SAME DESTINATION

It seems to me that there are two different ways around the "round barn" of learning a few chords which will ultimately get you to the same place. The problem is that 99% of the people fail going one way, while going around my way has proven enormously more successful (not to mention more fun) for the other 1%. I invite you to join the minority!

Route 1 (bad, bad, bad)
I've taught you how to build chords. Now, close the book and spend your time learning every chord type, starting on every root, working on being able to move from any one chord to any other chord with equal ease. Don't worry, it is only something like 100,000 different variations on which to work. Have fun! Probably an hour or two each day for the next four or five years, and you'll have it licked. When you get it all learned really well, come back, and then I will start teaching you how to use the chords in a tune.

Route 2 (good, good, good)

Please go out and get your very "mostest, favoritest, all-time hit paradist, I would feel I had lived a full life if I could play this tunist," piece of music. All kidding aside, it desperately needs to be that tune that has you saying, "If I could just sit down at a piano and play (fill in the blank)."

Run, don't walk, to a store where you can find some music, and buy that song. Don't worry about your pre-conceived notions of ease or difficulty. For example, "Ooh, look at all the notes! I could never play that tune" or "too many sharps or flats in that one." It doesn't matter, just make sure to buy *your* tune.

Now sit down and make a list of every chord symbol you find in the tune. You'll find them up above the lines of music (the staffs for you serious folk)! There will probably be five or six chords total (that's no science, you may have more or less) that end up repeating many times through the song.

Take that list, figure out the notes in the chords, and get them memorized. It may take you, what, an hour, maybe two at the most? Then read on, and I'll quickly show you how to put those chords to work playing your all-time fav' tune.

How's that! No "Book 1, Book 2, Book 3" drudgery. No immense cost of years of private piano lessons. No playing all these silly "kiddy" tunes for years until you have worked your way up the ladder enough that your teacher lets you play something that you really enjoy. Just a little bit of "hammering" through a few chords and then immediately working on the tune you have always dreamed about playing the most, FIRST.

NO PAIN, ALL GAIN

I cannot express how strongly I have found this strategy to be superior for people I have taught to play. For the umpteenth time, it comes down to the fact that unless you are having some fun and getting some immediate gratification playing piano, history proves to me that you are exceedingly likely to bail out and quit the effort (which has very likely happened to many of you previous to reading this book).

Is there some crime in having fun right away? You're just doing this for personal enrichment; so get that old mistaken notion out of your noggin that says "no pain, no gain." It might be right for building muscles but not for building piano playing skills.

To summarize, the way to work on chords is to learn ONLY those chords you need to learn to get through the tune on which you are currently working. And you also better make sure that the tune you are working on is one that really gets your juices flowing. Why waste time working an a tune you don't enjoy? Life is too short to play dumb tunes!

KEEP GOING SCOTT, YOU'RE ON A ROLL, MAKE IT EVEN EASIER!

I thought it was important to give you the in-depth explanation of how to figure out the notes in a chord using the "distance in half-steps" method I showed you in the previous sections. However, wouldn't it be nice if there was a handier and speedier way to look up what notes are in a chord? Well, there is…

Instead of figuring out one-by-one what the notes in a chord are, people over the years have developed a few very similar ways to show what a chord "looks" like visually with a diagram. They all in some way display a representation of a keyboard with some other representation of what notes need to be played to achieve that chord. The diagrams I have used so far are very typical, with dots on the notes that are to be played. For example, here is a D7 diagram denoting D, F#, A, and C in the chord.

D7

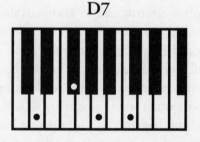

Where can you find these diagrams? A few different places. There have been a number of books published through the years that have all these diagrams in them for every significant chord type. On that note, there have also been some famous books published that have a gazillion chords in them, but which show them all notated in traditional music notation.

I'm not particularly fond of these books, however, because they make you go through the added step of mentally translating what the notation says into what the chord looks like on a keyboard under your fingers. I'd rather just skip that "translation" step and get right to what counts: what the chord looks like on a keyboard. You'll need to go to a music store and have them find one of the few that are available. (A word of experience here: they probably won't have any in stock because their main customers for piano material are traditional classical piano teachers who rarely condone using them because the books don't use music notation.)

THE KEYBOARD CHORD FINDER

A newer, much more convenient solution has been developed to give you all the chord diagrams you'll need. It is a small electronic device about the size of a deck of cards. It has buttons on it with all the roots and all the chord symbol variations. After you enter the root and what "flavor" you're looking for, it displays electronically a keyboard diagram for whatever chord symbol you have entered. They look just like the example diagrams I've used so far in the book (with dots over the keys to tell you which notes are in the chord). I find it much more convenient and quicker for looking up unknown chords due to its small size than having to leaf through a book with thousands of diagrams to find the one I need. It runs from a battery so there are no electrical cords or anything to deal with. I just leave it sitting at my piano. You just enter whatever chord you need, and it shows it to you immediately. Very handy. You can find more information about the keyboard chord finder at:

http://www.scottthepianoguy.com/chordfinder.html

CHAPTER 6

LET'S GET DOWN TO BUSINESS AND START PLAYING!

We now need to put both 1) the ability to read one note at a time in the treble clef, and 2) the fact that we can learn a few chords, to use in the real world. It's time to pull out some music and start giving it a little closer inspection. Typical piano sheet music looks something like this:

Rather than just looking at it as a whole and thinking "Whoa, that looks like that stuff that kept me from playing piano in the first place," let's dissect it into a few pieces to make it more manageable. Starting at the top above everything else, you see some letters, or (yup, you guessed it) CHORD SYMBOLS! Yippee!!! That is where you will always find chord symbols. They are always up above the lines of music. So, in this tune, the chords you would need to learn are C, F, and G7.

Right below the chord symbols you see boxes with lines and dots in them. Those are guitar chord charts which tell what finger to put on what string at which fret. As a piano player you can totally ignore them. Sometimes you won't find them in your music anyway.

A little rant coming up here... It always cracks me up when I have serious piano players give me grief about teaching chords using the chord diagrams I have suggested you use. They think it is somehow "not musically sound" since you are not using notation to learn your chords.

I always want to come back with "Well then, go talk to guitar players, because they get little diagrams actually printed right in the notation!"

It would be the equivalent of me coming out with a whole product line of sheet music that had our little chord diagrams printed right below every chord symbol. Hmmmm, now that's not a bad idea at all...

Below the chord symbols and guitar chord charts is the traditional music notation. You see that there are two sets of five lines (the staffs). The top set is the treble clef (because it has that curvy "S" symbol at the beginning) and the lower set is the bass clef (because it has the backward "C" symbol at the beginning).

We'll be paying close attention to the treble clef (top); however, in the unbelievably good news department, YOU CAN TOTALLY (yes, I said totally) IGNORE THE BASS CLEF. Just to keep you doing cartwheels out of joy for the next few moments, I'll reiterate: You will <u>never</u> have to read the bass clef ever again. Yeee hah!!!!!

So to summarize, out of all the gobbledy-gook that makes up traditional piano sheet music, all you need to pay attention to are the chord symbols and the notes in the treble staff. You can totally ignore <u>everything</u> else.

THE "SCOTT BLINDERS"

By putting on these imaginary goggles (The Scott Blinders) that magically block out everything but what you need to be concerned with, it turns this:

into this:

That's a little easier on the eyes, huh? Take a look at a few different pieces of music and get used to ignoring 90% of it. It's a pretty enjoyable skill to acquire. (It makes you feel down-right sneaky, doesn't it?)

"LEAD" ME ON...TO LEAD SHEETS

What we are actually doing by ignoring everything but the chord symbols and the treble clef is turning traditional music notation into the kind of notation that pros use. It is called **Lead Sheet Notation**. That's right, a lead sheet. Simply put, a lead sheet shows a single-note-at-a-time melody line in the treble clef, with chord symbols up above it. No matter what the tune or style (assuming it is not classical music), it all is notated in exactly the same way: a one note melody line with chord symbols.

If your sheet music does not have chord symbols in it, you can not use it in this style. However, the great news is that probably 95% of non-classical sheet music ever printed does have chord symbols in it. So, have faith that you can always turn a normal piece of sheet music into a lead sheet by simply ignoring everything but the chord symbols and melody line as we did previously.

Stop and think about this for a minute. You're probably thinking "You mean to tell me that *every* tune in this style is just a one note melody line with a few chord symbols?" Yes, that is exactly what I'm saying. As long as you get to the point where you can read a one-note-at-a-time sequence of notes in the treble clef, you're done from a note reading standpoint. Done, finished, finité, all over.

I have just given you the freedom to take off the chains that hold down the vast majority of wannabe piano players: that is, the perceived need to keep working forever and ever on becoming a great note reader. That mistaken notion just got obliterated. You have a very finite goal that you must reach (which, by the way, even if you can't read a single note yet is only a few days down the road), but once you do, you're done. You will have all the note reading skills you need to play any tune ever written. This lead sheet notation is like the great equalizer. Within a very fine boundary, no tune is easier or harder than any other, because they are all notated the same way: one note at a time.

Let me mention one more thing regarding the melody line. I keep saying "one note at a time" melody line. When you are using our imaginary goggles (Scott Blinders) to block out 90% of a normally notated piece of music, you may sometimes find that the sheet music has multiple notes (chords) played at the same time in the treble clef. If that ever happens, you simply play the highest note and ignore the others below it. The uppermost note is always the melody note.

WHAT'S FAKE ABOUT A FAKE BOOK?

I now have even more good news to bestow on you. *They actually print lead sheets in their native format!* Now you don't even have to go through the step of ignoring 90% of regular notation. You can get sheet music that is notated directly in lead sheet format (i.e. one note melody line in the treble clef with chord symbols above it). Where do you find lead sheets? In something called a *fake book*.

There is absolutely nothing fake about a fake book. A fake book is simply a big giant collection of lead sheets. That's it. Fake books usually tend to focus on a particular style of music. There are jazz fake books, Broadway show tune fake books, country fake books, pop/rock fake books, Christmas fake books, even sacred fake books (that last one usually gets a chuckle). Again, all they are is a large collection of lead sheets in one book. Not only is there nothing fake about them, but they are what pros use. Pros don't read sheet music, they read lead sheets (which are found in fake books.)

When's the last time you saw a piano player out working a gig reading a piece of sheet music? Never, right? It's because if we did read sheet music, we would never get hired again because we would sound so corny. Instead we play non-classical tunes stylistically correctly by reading a lead sheet to learn the tune.

You can find fake books at printed music stores and at some really large traditional bookstores. You can also find some fake books through the web. Come to www.scotthouston.com and you can find some links to a bunch of fake books I personally recommend.

Here's another "museum of the obvious" comment: What makes a fake book right for you is whether or not it has tunes in it you like. End of story. Find a book that has lots of tunes in it that you like, in a style that you enjoy.

OKAY, I'M STARTING TO BUY INTO THIS

Let's take stock of where we are so far. You know that all you'll ever need to read is a one note melody line in the treble clef. You also know how to decipher chord symbols found up above the melody line. You can learn what notes the chords have in them by using the chart in Chapter 4 and counting up the half-steps. Even better (or at least easier and faster) you could get a chord finder and just see what they look like in a keyboard diagram. You know that the way to learn your chords is not to spend the foreseeable future trudging through practicing every chord known to mankind, but instead to simply learn the few chords that are in the tune on which you are currently working. By the way, you better make sure that the tune you are working on is an all-time favorite of yours so that you'll be darned motivated to play it ASAP! Now let's put it all together...

You need to think of a lead sheet as two separate entities: one, the sequence of chord symbols, and two, the notes in the melody line. As simplistic as this seems, all you do to play a lead sheet is play the chord symbols with your left hand, and play the one note melody line with your right hand. I'm going to give you some more detailed guidelines coming right up, but please don't lose sight of the bigger picture. Chords with your left hand, melody line with your right. Next, I will give you some very basic guidelines to form a strong foundation for this style of playing using lead sheets. However, please know that what I will be describing is the minimum you need to get started. If you feel like playing more than what I am describing, go right ahead.

Remember, there is only one person you are doing this for – yourself. So let your own ears be the judge. If it sounds good to you, then it's correct. If not, try something else! You're the final authority in this arena. Not me, not some piano teacher, not your family. YOU!

LEFT HAND FIRST

No, I'm not starting a rousing round of the hokey-pokey. I am going to look at this whole process and mentally split it in two pieces: what is the left hand's job and what is the right hand's job.

Let's work on the left hand/chords first. A great rule of thumb is that at a minimum, you need to play a chord at the beginning of every measure. Nothing technical here, just make sure you are playing a chord with your left hand every time you get to a new measure and hold the keys down until you play the next chord.

A quick word about the way some lead sheets are notated: If you ever get to a measure in a lead sheet (or your sheet music which you are ignoring 90% of) which does not have any chord symbol up above it, you simply repeat the chord symbol from the previous measure. Simple. If whoever printed the lead sheet was very fastidious, there probably won't be any "blank" measures. However, since this kind of notation was developed by players themselves, it has not always been an exact science. It has kind of evolved throughout the years. Some notators in this style follow the convention that says "just keep playing the same chord until I give you another one" which results in a measure with no chord symbol at all. On this same topic, that is why you will sometimes see chord symbols spelled out differently, which I mentioned in the earlier chapter about chord symbols. For example, Cm instead of Cmin, or Fmaj7 instead of FM7. This lead sheet notation is a living breathing thing that keeps evolving as time marches on. So just remember to at least play a chord at the beginning of every new measure and hold the keys down until you play the next chord.

What about the situation where there is more than one chord symbol in a measure? Well, for fear of sounding obvious, you play them all. You will always find the chord symbol given to you directly above the beat (or the melody note) where it should fall in the measure. So concentrate on your melody line and whenever a new chord symbol appears above a note, make sure to play it with that note. Again, your ears will blatantly be able to tell you if you are doing it wrong or right. Trust them.

RIGHT HAND NEXT

Now let's discuss the right hand. Your right hand's primary and by far most important role is to play the one-note-at-a-time melody line. Anything else that gets played is just icing on the cake. I think a good way to think of it is as though your right hand is the solo, and your left hand chords are the accompaniment.

I often get questions about fingering from very concerned looking ex-piano students, who try this style for the first time. They say, "What fingers should we use?" or something like "Should I put numbers under the notes to tell me what fingers to use?" (I suppose you could get little number tattoos on the tops of your fingers that you can see all the time to make that a decent strategy. Whatever works, I guess ...) Seriously, the issue of fingering is very important when studying classical music because playing that style is an exercise in perfection. But for our purposes, it doesn't matter one iota how you finger something as long as you're getting it played. No one cares how you finger a piece of music, they just care how you play it. Never once in my life has someone come up to me after playing in public and said, "Boy oh boy Scott, your fingering was great tonight!" What I hope is that they will come up and say, "Scott, you sure *sounded* great tonight."

So for the issue of fingering, remember this: There is nothing on a piano that should <u>ever</u> have your hands all twisted and contorted. Everything on the piano is right out in front of you and should be able to be played without being a contortionist. If you ever feel like a contortionist (at least of the hands) then take a look at what you are doing fingering-wise because there will be an easier answer. Again, for fear of sounding like a simpleton, let logic rule in this department. If something is getting your hands in some odd-ball position, take a minute to find an easier position that isn't as awkward. Know that there is a simpler way out there, because nothing should ever cause you to get all tied up in a knot on a piano.

It all gets down to what the "end game" is for any activity. For this activity, playing non-classical piano, the end game is to sound good and have fun. Period. All of the minutiae that piano players tend to go through when taking classical lessons like fingerings, or figuring out key signatures, or counting out rhythms (remember 1-ee-and-ah, 2-ee-and-ah and all of that... jeez) are just roadblocks in our path toward sounding good as soon as possible and having fun immediately. All of those things will come to you through *playing*, not *practicing*. If you never get to playing something you want to play and enjoy playing, all of that won't matter anyway because you'll quit! You must start playing immediately so that you'll have the desire to keep on with your efforts. Then your playing will naturally lead you to all those other things in fair time as your desire to improve continues to grow. On the other hand, if you never get off the ground to begin with, all of the other stuff is for naught. So don't waste your time or effort on that stuff now. Just go play and have fun.

NOW PUT IT ALL TOGETHER

So to summarize the basic way to interpret a lead sheet on the piano, you will:

- **Play at least one chord per measure with your left hand**
    - you know what chord to play based on the chord symbols
    - if there is more than one chord per measure, play them (duh...)

- **Play the one note melody line with your right hand.**
    - make sure NOT to play it exactly as written or you will be doomed to sound like a corny sheet music player
    - instead feel free to "noodle around" until it sounds good to YOU

- **Put them together**

Congratulations! You are well on your way to sounding like a pro. You are now playing non-classical music stylistically correctly, rather than incorrectly using the rules of classical piano.

⸳⸴ a Flash!

How to Lose All Respect for Piano Players in One Easy Chapter

This chapter title comes from the fact that we are going to delve into a bunch of techniques for taking your piano playing to the next level, beyond the very basic guidelines I have given you in the last section.

Another, probably more honest way to think of these techniques is that these are just a bunch of well worn sneaky tricks that pianists have been using for years to dupe people into thinking they are better than they are. But hey, I'm not above using sneaky tricks if it gets me closer to the end game of sounding good playing the piano So, let's dig in!

THE IMPORTANCE OF LISTENING & IMITATING

After all of these different ideas, you will find an Internet web address that you can go to to hear an audio sample of what it sounds like played by a true master (that would be me, of course…). All kidding aside, I strongly suggest that you go listen to these audio clips because, as in most things musical, it is difficult to put these examples into words to describe them fully. All the instructions you need (computer-wise) to hear these examples from your computer can be found on the site as well.

If you are more interested in getting all of these examples on an audio CD, go to:

http://www.scottthepianoguy.com/book/cd.html

It is also worth noting that it is practically impossible to notate these different tricks in traditional music notation. In many cases there is no traditional way to notate the nuances needed to express the correct way to play these ideas. It is for this reason that I am not showing the ideas notated in traditional music notation.

Trying to "read" many of these ideas in notation will only intimidate those of you who aren't very proficient note readers. For those of you who do read pretty well, I fear you will feel compelled to play them the way they are notated, rather than the way they should be played.

The best technique is to *hear* them for yourself. Then imitate them. One more time… listen, then imitate.

IDEAS FOR YOUR LEFT HAND:

Rolled chords

One very simple technique is to "roll" whatever chord you are playing in your left hand when you play it. What I mean is to start with the lowest note and very quickly in succession roll upward with your hand playing the other notes in the chord until they are all being held down. Please understand that your hand position doesn't have to change at all. You still can think of the chord as one "shape" under your fingers. Just don't play all the notes at exactly the same time. Very quickly play them in succession from the lowest to the highest note in the chord.

http://www.scottthepianoguy.com/book/examples/rolled.html

Multiple chords

This technique involves repeating your chord(s) in a steady rhythm with your left hand more than just one chord per measure. For example, instead of just hitting your chord and holding it the whole measure until the next chord symbol appears, you could repeat the chord twice in each measure. Or maybe three or four times per measure... Don't forget that you still need to change to another chord whenever a new chord symbol comes down the pike. Just because you are having some more activity in your left hand doesn't mean that you can forget to keep your eyes on when the chord changes from one symbol to the next.

http://www.scottthepianoguy.com/book/examples/multiple.html

Rhythmic pattern for chords

Taking the previous technique a little further, how about playing some repeating rhythmic pattern with your left hand chords? There are hundreds to choose from, but what is more important is that you tend to stick with the same pattern for at least a few measures at a time. Listen to the example for a few commonly used patterns.

http://www.scottthepianoguy.com/book/examples/pattern.html

Root first, then rest of chord

Another way to make your left hand playing a little more interesting is to separate the chord into two pieces: the root and the rest of the chord. To refresh your memory, the root is the single note identified by the letter (plus a sharp or flat if there is one immediately following) at the beginning of a chord symbol. The idea here is to play the root first by itself, and then follow it up with the rest of the notes in the chord on a subsequent beat. For example if the chord was a Cmaj7 (in which the four notes are C, E, G, B) you would play a C (the root) on the first beat wherever the chord symbol appeared, and then you would play E, G, B together (the rest of the chord) on the next beat (or some subsequent beat as long as you did it consistently on each different chord).

Like the techniques before this one, this just gives you a little more "oomph" to spice up your left hand chord playing. It also is much easier to hear than it is to describe, so check out the example here:

http://www.scottthepianoguy.com/book/examples/rootfirst.html

Root octave down

Taking the above example to the next level, how about playing the root one octave lower than where you are playing the rest of your chord? (An octave is the key with the same name twelve half steps lower or higher. Even simpler than counting twelve half-steps, just find the next key down that "looks" exactly the same position-wise. Because a keyboard just keeps repeating itself over and over every twelve keys, just find the same "looking" key in the adjacent repeated set.) Then you need to "jump up" the octave to play the rest of the chord. This one is a little tougher due to "target practice" reasons. It comes down to this consistent left hand motion of jumping down one octave to the root, then jumping back up to play the rest of the chord. Also, if it is easier for you, you can actually play the entire chord, including the root, when you come back up from playing the root by itself down one octave. Just work on your left hand by itself as slowly as needed to get the target practice down to a point where you can successfully hit the note you are reaching for when you jump down to get the root.

I also want to mention the pedals for the first time. One thing that will make this technique sound smoother is to use the sustain pedal. The sustain pedal is the pedal on the right when using a traditional acoustic piano. If you have an electronic, or digital, piano you might only have one pedal, which is the sustain. The idea is to press down the pedal when you play the single root down one octave. Then hold the pedal down while you come up and play the chord. You can keep the pedal down until right before you play the next single root down one octave. At that point, you lift the pedal up and press it down again when you have the next root played. Just keep repeating that cycle through the tune.

This keeps the notes sounding while your hand is jumping back and forth from root to chord. It smooths out the sound and makes it not as "jumpy" or detached.

Now to contradict myself, sometimes it is interesting to sound kind of detached, or what musicians call "staccato." If so, just don't use the pedal. Simple enough. Remember, as always, YOUR ear is the guide. If you like the way it sounds, it's right. If not, do it another way. It's your time. It's your effort. Do what YOU like. There is no absolute right or wrong in this style of piano.

http://www.scottthepianoguy.com/book/examples/octavedown.html

Root alone

After the last one, this one will seem like a breeze, but it can be very effective as a "change of pace" in a tune. All that this one entails is playing only the root, never the full chord. This also works better down one or two octaves from where you normally play your chords. You just play the single root note wherever the chord change occurs, nothing else. It is most effectively used as a "breath of fresh air" after you have been playing some other way for a while.

http://www.scottthepianoguy.com/book/examples/rootalone.html

*T*here is a common phrase among jazz musicians, "less is more." What it refers to is the fact that many times, less (but more strategically played) notes are in better taste than just force feeding as many notes as possible down a listener's ear. There is a tendency among musicians to always try and play right up to their technical ability. It is like every time they play they feel the need to impress you with every bit of technical prowess they can possibly muster. More notes, played faster, in less time, etc. In reality, the great ones may have that ability within their reach, but they rarely display it, preferring instead to play things more modestly and pleasing to the ear. That way, when they do pull out their bag of "super-dooper" tricks, it is even more impressive and awe-inspiring.

*T*he reason I bring up this "less is more" idea here is that I encourage you to try things like this "root alone" technique from time to time. There is nothing in better taste than to vary your playing with not only more notes and intensity and other things, but also with less of the same things. This technique is a great example of that. Remembering "less is more" will serve you well your entire musical life.

*A*s an additional note on this topic, in the singing world I have two great examples of less is more: Tony Bennett and Frank Sinatra. Even if you're not a fan of these two or their styles, you cannot escape the conclusion that they were/are masters of the idea of less is more. Neither of them sings a plethora of notes, but the well selected ones that they do sing are beautifully and masterfully appropriate.

Root and fifth

This one deals with playing a very simple two note pattern in your left hand instead of the chord. The two notes are the root and seven half steps above the root. That second note is often referred to as the "fifth" because it is five notes up from the root in a major scale. Don't worry if you don't know about scales. Just count up seven half steps from the root and it will give you the second note. For example, in a C chord the two notes are C and G. In an Fmin chord the two notes are F and C. In a D#7 chord the two notes are a D# and an A#. You just use the root and the note seven half steps above the root. You will find that in almost every case, your pinky and thumb of your left hand will very comfortably fall onto the two notes.

Although you could do it differently if you wanted, the pattern you usually play with these two notes is: root in the first half of the measure, fifth in the second half of the measure. Back and forth, root and fifth, root and fifth. About the only hard rule I can give you on this is to always play the root whenever the chord symbol changes. In other words, make sure that the first thing someone hears in your left hand when a chord symbol changes is the root of the chord.

http://www.scottthepianoguy.com/book/examples/rootfifth.html

Arpeggios

Just sounds hard, doesn't it? A-r-p-e-g-g-i-o… Although this is something practiced feverishly in classical piano studies, it also is used extensively in our style of playing. An arpeggio is a chord that is being played note by note instead of all at once. It is similar to the rolled chord technique we discussed earlier, except it is a gazillion (wow, that's a lot…) times slower and more deliberate.

For example, let's look at playing an arpeggio of a D7 chord. That chord has these four notes: D, F#, A, and C. Instead of playing all four of the notes together at the beginning of a measure, I would play each of them one at a time on each beat from the lowest to the highest, i.e., D, then F#, then A, then C. Then if the chord stays the same I would do it over again, or if it changes I would switch to the next chord and play the notes one at a time.

Please keep in mind that your hand position doesn't change at all doing this versus playing the chord all at once. It is not like you need to learn a whole new position or anything else sneaky or difficult. You are simply going to play your fingers one at a time instead of all at once.

This creates a nice kind of "flowing" feeling to your left hand playing. You can hear an example of it here:

http://www.scottthepianoguy.com/book/examples/arpeggio.html

IDEAS FOR YOUR RIGHT HAND

Playing the melody line in octaves

This technique is fun to try because it will sound so familiar to you. This is used like crazy by piano players, particularly when playing slower tunes (like ballads). All you do is play every note in the melody line, but at the same time add the same note one octave higher. The best way to do it is with your thumb and pinky. For every note in the melody line, play it simultaneously with your thumb and with your pinky one octave higher, resulting in the entire line being played in octaves.

If you have a hard time stretching your hand far enough apart to do this, great news! It is actually better sounding to play your thumb just slightly in front of your pinky anyway. So just "rock" your hand from the thumb up to your pinky, playing the lower note just barely ahead of the higher note. Again, remember that this one is great for ballads. It is a really pretty way to play melodies. Here's what it sounds like:

http://www.scottthepianoguy.com/book/examples/octaves.html

Filling in other chord tones

This technique is a little more advanced, simply because it requires that you be very familiar with the notes in whatever chord you are playing with your left hand. The trick to this one is to play almost all of the melody line with the pinky of your right hand. If you do that, you will then have your first four fingers feeling left out and looking for a little action, right? Well, what you can do with them is fill in, or double, any notes that are in the chord that you are playing with your left hand. Let me give you a quick example...

Say in your tune you are playing a C7 chord with your left hand, and the melody note happens to be on an E. Using this technique, you would be playing the E with your pinky. Then you could, in any combination or variation, use your other free fingers to also play any of the notes in a C7 chord (which are C, E, G, and Bb). Just to give you a concrete finish to this example, you could play your thumb on a G and your index finger on a Bb. So, your right hand would be playing G, Bb, and E (the melody note) along with your left hand playing the C7 chord as usual.

The effect of this one is to "fill out" or "broaden" the sound of your playing simply because you are playing more notes. Please understand, however, that there is no hard and fast rule for this technique regarding playing chord tones with every melody note. It is just a way to kind of fill things in here and there. Listen to the audio example as I fill in chord tones on quite a few melody notes that I play.

http://www.scottthepianoguy.com/book/examples/upoctave.html

Play the melody line up one or two octaves

This one is so blatantly simple it might not even seem to be worth mentioning. However, I know that some of you who are fastidious note readers (you know who you are – come on, fess up) have a tremendously hard time not feeling like you MUST play whatever is written. Well, take off those chains, my friends!

Many times it sounds great to simply play the entire melody line up one or two octaves from where it is notated in the sheet music (or lead sheet if you've wised up and gotten a fake book). Nothing tricky here. It certainly doesn't make anything tougher to read because once you've started, it is all relative. Just find the first note of the melody line up one octave from where it is written, and then continue to play the line in that higher octave; it is sometimes just easier to hear the melody, and it sounds nicer up there. As always, let your ear be the guide. If you like it, do it. If you don't, don't do it.

http://www.scottthepianoguy.com/book/examples/upoctave.html

Two or three note "run-up"

Here is a little trick that really makes your playing start to sound professional.

Instead of just "landing" right on a melody note, "run up" to it from two or three half steps below it. For example, if the melody note you need to play is a C, play as fast as you can an A, A#, and B right before finishing on the C. I mean really fast, too.

This may take a little work on your part to get your fingers working correctly. The great news is I can give you a little drill to do that doesn't require you sitting in front of a keyboard. You can do this whenever and wherever you want… at work, in your car while driving, on your dog's head (Nick, my dog, really loves me practicing this on him).

We'll start with something all of us do naturally. Lay your right hand casually on a table face down (I guess that would be palm down…) and tap your fingers rapidly in succession from your pinky to your thumb. It should be this very smooth, very fast, very rhythmic sound. Ba-da-da-da-da. You know, the way you do when you're in your car behind the wheel: impatient, late, and in a hurry, waiting for a light to change. There are your fingers on the steering wheel practicing piano and you didn't even know it! Ba-da-da-da-da. Ba-da-da-da-da. Ba-da-da-da-da. Green light! Vroooooom…

OK, now here's the kicker. You need to do it backward. From your thumb to your pinky, not from your pinky to your thumb. "WHAT?" you say, "That is unnatural!" I know it feels really weird at first because our hands so naturally will do the "pinky to thumb" thing. But if you'll notice the name of this technique it is called a "run up" not "run down" so we need to get smooth with our right hand doing it in reverse, from the thumb up to the pinky. When it sounds just as smooth and rhythmic going up as it does coming down, you've got it.

As an aside . . .

Lest the ASPCA get all over me for the previous "practicing on my dog Nick" comment, I encourage you to try practicing this on top of your pet's noggin. It puts Nick into a state of deep relaxation as I lightly tap my "Ba-da-da-da-da" rhythm into his subconscious. It must be some sort of doggy-alpha-wave thing. Who knows... Anyway, I can judge the quality of my technique by how far out of his mouth his tongue hangs as he gets more and more relaxed. More hang = better technique.

Now to apply the "two or three note run-up technique" to the example I mentioned of running up to C. I would probably put my thumb on the A, index finger on the A#, middle finger on the B, and finally play the melody note with my fourth finger on the C. Just run it up as quickly as you can. Imagine trying to emulate the way a trombone player can slide smoothly up to a note by pulling in on a slide, as opposed to having to play distinct notes. That is kind of the effect you are trying to emulate even though you are constrained by having to play distinct separate notes since you can't bend a note on a piano.

You tend to use this "run-up" trick when you are at the beginning of a phrase (a hoity-toity way to say group of notes). For example, sing "Jingle Bells" to yourself (do this quietly if there are people around you ... especially if it is summer when you are reading this). You could "run up" to the first "Jing," but you probably want to play the following two "gle" and "Bells" melody notes by themselves without the "run-up."

Another note to mention (pardon the pun) is that you don't always have to use exactly four notes to run up. You can use more or fewer (although if you use more than five you must be an alien with more fingers than the rest of us). A three-note run-up is just fine too. A two-note run-up is actually just a kind of sloppy grace note, which is great as well.

Here is the example audio clip:

http://www.scottthepianoguy.com/book/examples/runup.html

The "King of the Run-Up" (although I'm not sure he knows it) is a great player/writer/producer named Jeff Lorber. Listen to any of his right hand keyboard playing, and you'll get a giant dose, over and over, of the "run-up" in use. In fact, now that I mention it, I would suggest that you listen to Jeff's right hand playing for great examples of all sorts of things you can do to make your melody line playing more interesting. His style fits into the wishy-washy category of "smooth jazz/new age/funk/R&B/etc." but he tends to play a right hand keyboard line as a solo instrument by playing the melody line alone as the lead instrument you hear. For that reason it is pretty easy to pick up some of the things he is doing because it is so "out front" in the mix. Even if you don't particularly like that style, he's a master at playing interesting melody lines. I love his playing in that regard. Check out **www.scottthepianoguy.com/jefflorber.html** *for some info on his recordings.*

Playing chords in empty spots

This final technique I am going to describe is probably the most technically difficult. That is because it entails picking up your right hand from where it is playing the melody line, moving up the keyboard to play some things, and then coming back down to play some more of the melody line all in a very short amount of time. In other words, the "target practice" factor is higher in this one than in most.

The idea is to take advantage of "dead spots" in the melody line—that is, wherever there are some lulls in the melody line, and your right hand is sitting idly by waiting for another melody note to come down the pike. When that occurs, you can put that idle time to use by playing chords, or some variation of a chord like an arpeggio, an octave or two higher than the melody line with your otherwise idle right hand. The trick is making sure you get back to playing the melody line when it is time, because without question the melody line is the priority here. This technique is just a little "icing on the cake" to add some more interest and depth to your playing. If you fail to play the melody line, however, the whole house of cards will come tumbling down.

Some different ideas for what to do during these lulls include:
• Playing exactly what your left hand is playing, just up an octave or two higher
• Playing the same chord as the left hand, but as separate notes, going either up or down
• Doing a sequence of arpeggios of the chord, up or down two or three octaves
• Playing the root of the chord in octaves up high on the keyboard (like "bells")

There is really no limit to the possibilities here. The idea is just to fill in some of the otherwise dead spots with something else in the right hand. Another way to think of it is that you are "accompanying" your own melody line by playing some things when the melody is silent. As usual, your best bets as to what to play revolve around the notes in the chord you are currently playing with your left hand.

http://www.scottthepianoguy.com/book/examples/chordsempty.html

THREE CHORDS & YOU'RE DONE—
THE BLUES

I could not think about writing this book without including a section on the Blues because it...

1) is the biggest single influence on popular music.
2) forms the basis for many different musical styles we hear every day.
3) is some of the most fun you will ever have playing.
4) is super easy to start playing.
5) has at its basis only three chords.

What am I talking about? The blues, man, the blues!

Now before you go scurrying off saying to yourself, "I don't like blues music. I'm going to skip this section. It always reminds me of big unshaven guitar players in dark smoky late night bars. Sick, sick, sick..." Let me implore you to stick around for just a few more sentences.

Yes, there is a common image of blues bands, which either repels or appeals to a lot of people; however, there is an undeniable fact that the vast majority of non-classical music we hear has somewhere in its roots a heritage that stems from the blues. Blues is the "primordial ooze" from which almost all non-classical music was born. If you look deep into the "DNA" of any style of non-classical music, whether it be rock, jazz standards, country, gospel, Broadway show tunes, whatever... you will find traces of the blues.

WHY THERE ARE SO MANY BLUES BANDS OUT THERE

Enough with the science talk, let's get to the good stuff. Here is some great news about the blues for us chord-style piano players. In its simplest form, the blues has only three chords in it. That's right, three: C, F, and G

I'm not kidding. If you can learn the C, F, and G chords you can spend literally hundreds of hours having fun, sounding good, amazing your friends and family, contemplating quitting your day job (whoa there, Nellie, not quite so fast...). All you need are three chords, a decent PA system, an old van in which to haul your gear, and you're in biz! Now you know why there are so many blues bands out there.

THE PROGRESSION IS THE COMMON THREAD

So if there are only three chords, the game becomes when to switch from one to another. Here is the way it works: The blues is a twelve measure chord progression that simply repeats over and over. The twelve measures have three chords in them that must be played in the following pattern:

4 measures of C
2 measures of F
2 measures of C
1 measure of G
1 measure of F
2 measures of C

Now I personally think it is easier to think of the blues as three sets of four measures rather than twelve individual measures. Thinking of it that way you have:

Set 1: 4 C's
Set 2: 2 F's, 2 C's
Set 3: 1 G, 1 F, 2 C's

Once you've played the twelve measures you just repeat it ad infinitum. Congratulations, you now know the blues. Seriously—that is it! Twelve measures in that particular chord order, repeated indefinitely. Next...

THE "BLUES BUFFET"

Now that you know what the blues is and what its form is, you need to learn a few patterns you can use in both your hands. This is where I like to think of it as a "blues buffet." The "blues buffet" is this never-ending supply of patterns for either your right hand or your left hand. Once you learn a pattern in one chord (C, for example), you just need to physically move your hand position to the other two chords (F & G) whenever you get to them in the blues progression. Same pattern, just started on a different root.

The reason I refer to it as a buffet is that you can order any right hand pattern. Then choose any left hand pattern. Put it all on the same buffet plate and find that it will sound (taste) great! Because all the patterns follow the same chord progression, they all sound great together. It's like "Garanimals" (sorry Sears. . .) for blues pianists. You never need to worry about your patterns not matching.

There is no set right or wrong way to play the blues (assuming you are following the cardinal rule of the twelve measures in their particular order). Just a few of the unlimited options are:

- Chords with your left, pattern with your right
- Pattern with your left, chords with your right
- Chords with your left, chords with your right
- Chords with your left, improvised line with your right
- Walking bass line with your left, chords with your right
- Walking bass line with your left, improvised line with your right

See what I mean? Totally mix and match.

It obviously is way beyond the scope of this book to get into a huge description of all of the wonderful nuances that make up the blues. But on the following pages I do want to give you just a taste of a few patterns to whet your appetite.

Unlike the tricks in the last chapter, I *will* show these blues patterns notated since you will need to know the particular notes I am using. However, I am only going to notate the pattern as you would play it in C. I will use the bass clef for left hand patterns and the treble clef for right hand patterns. (I will also put the names of the notes directly below them in case you're having a problem reading them.)

It is important for you to realize that you need to focus on the *pattern* here, not the notation. You'll then need to transfer the pattern starting on an F and then on a G when needed. I'm not trying to shortchange you. To the contrary, by allowing you to focus on only the patterns for the F and G sections on your own, you will see them as they truly are – patterns, rather than incorrectly memorizing them as some exact notation.

In addition (and more importantly), I will also give you an Internet address where you can find an audio example of the pattern being explained and played appropriately. Please use the audio examples as the guide, not the notation. Traditional notation is simply not equipped to properly "record" this style of music. The only way to "get it" properly is to hear it and imitate it.

Lest you think I'm "cheating," trust me when I say listening and imitating is the way this music has been passed down from its very inception.

A FEW LEFT HAND BLUES PATTERNS

C   E   G   E G

This first left hand pattern will probably sound really familiar to you. It basically just takes the major chord and splits it into its three separate notes. Then it repeats the top two before jumping back down to the root to repeat.

http://www.scottthepianoguy.com/book/examples/blues1.html

C   E   G   E

This one again splits a major chord into its three separate notes, goes up and then back down the chord. Very simple!

http://www.scottthepianoguy.com/book/examples/blues2.html

C   C   D   E   G

This could be considered a very basic version of what is called "walking" a bass line. Listen to what jazz bass players do in a small group setting to get a feel for this style of bass line. Imagine standing behind an upright bass rather than sitting at a piano when you play this, and you'll start to get the idea.

http://www.scottthepianoguy.com/book/examples/blues3.html

C   E   G   A   B♭   A   G   E

This one is just another variation of "walking" a bass line up and down some pattern that has the chord tones in it. You'll see that six out of the eight notes in this two measure pattern are simply a C7 chord (C, E, G, B♭.) In addition, an A note is put in there to make a smoother transition up and down between the G and B♭ notes.

http://www.scottthepianoguy.com/book/examples/blues4.html

B♭
G
E
C

How about playing a repeating rhythmic pattern with your left hand chord? Great idea... Try to imagine what a horn section would be doing in a big band to hear this one correctly –
          Baaah, bop   Baaah, bop

(What the heck is Baaah, bop? Now you know why listening to the examples is a good idea)

http://www.scottthepianoguy.com/book/examples/blues5.html

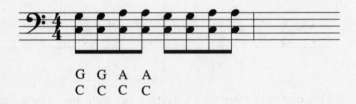

G G A A
C C C C

This one is FUN, FUN, FUN! You need to play this an octave lower than what I have notated to make it sound "appropriate" on the piano. This is kind of the "Granddaddy" of the blues shuffle bass patterns. When you play a shuffle, to really make it swing you need to emphasize the notes that are directly on the beat, and kind of de-emphasize every other note that falls between the beats. You'll hear it clearly on the example.

Also, take notice of the fact that none of these should be played rhythmically exactly as notated. Instead, you should "swing" the eighth notes rather than play them perfectly even. Kind of think – Ba da Ba da Ba da Ba da ... rather than dun, dun, dun, dun ...

Again, notation just doesn't work for these examples, you need to hear them and imitate what you are hearing.

http://www.scottthepianoguy.com/book/examples/blues6.html

This example opens a barn door (much broader than this book can deal with effectively) to a concept called "voicings." In its simplest form, a voicing is just a particular, specific order in which you play the notes of a chord. In a voicing you often don't even play all the notes in a chord, omitting some chord tones. Different voicings tend to make your ear "lean" toward a particular style or genre of music. This is due to the fact that different styles tend to have particular voicings that are used consistently to give the music that particular "flavor."

The three chord voicings I've given you above are very

"hip" and "jazzy" modern sounding voicings to use for the three different chords in the blues. Since none of these three voicings has the root on the bottom, they will sound even better if you first reach down an octave or two and play the root you are on, hold it with the sustain pedal, then come up and play the notes I've given you.

(In the interest of full disclosure, the three voicings above are actually a C9, F13, and G13 [instead of just plain old C, F, and G]. Makes you feel jazzy just thinking about it, doesn't it? Tee, hee, hee. Boy, will your friends and family be impressed when you play these voicings and sound very hip and in the know, then off-handedly mutter under your breath "*It's all about the 13th chords...*")

Again, listen to the example to get the gist of what this example sounds like.

http://www.scottthepianoguy.com/book/examples/blues7.html

A FEW RIGHT HAND BLUES PATTERNS

The majority of the time when you are playing the blues, your right hand is doing one of three things:

1. playing the melody of the tune
2. playing the three blues chords above a left hand bass pattern
3. improvising a melodic line above left hand chords

Number one on the list, playing the melody line, is self-explanatory and is what we've already covered earlier in the book.

I'm going to load you up with one good example you can use for situations numbers two and three. Just as before, an internet address where you can go to hear an audio example is given directly below the notation.

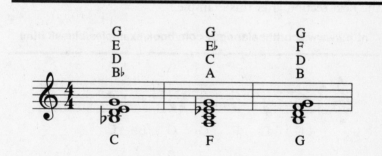

Similar to the last left hand example a few pages ago, here is another example of what are called chord "voicings." These are three right hand voicings you can use when you are playing some pattern in your left hand. Don't forget a voicing doesn't necessarily contain every note in a chord. That's why, for example, there isn't a C note in the first "C" chord example.

Just to reiterate, it doesn't matter what left hand pattern you play with these voicings. Just as long as you are switching the C, F, and G voicings at the appropriate time to make sure your right and left hands are in sync (i.e., on the same chord at the same time), it will all sound fine. So feel free to experiment a little and prove to yourself how fun the blues can be due to the "blues buffet" concept I mentioned earlier, where any right hand ideas can go with any left hand ideas. If it sounds good to you, it's correct. If not, try some other combination.

You also certainly do not need to hold the chords down in this right hand example for an entire measure at a time. Feel free to experiment with playing these chords in some rhythmic pattern within the measures. Again, just don't ever lose sight of where you are in the chord progression so that you always know when to change to the next chord. The technique is called "comping" and is discussed in more detail in the next section after this example.

http://www.scottthepianoguy.com/book/examples/blues8.html

C   E♭   F   G♭   G   B♭   C

This example may well turn out to be one of the greatest "nuggets" of information you will unearth in this book. The six different notes you see in the example above make up one of the sneakiest, easiest, most often played musical devices used in the blues genre. Its formal name is the "Blues Scale."

It is simply a six note scale. You can play it anywhere you want on a piano. Most of the time it is used to improvise a melody with your right hand while your left hand plays either chords or a pattern. You don't need to play it sequentially, or always up, or always down. The notes can be played in any order, anywhere you want to play them—up, down, inside out, whatever...

As an aside . . .

I should mention that the blues scale I have given you in this example is the "C" blues scale (as opposed to a blues scale built on a different root). Keep in mind that everything we have been talking about concerning the blues has been assuming that you would be playing in the key of C. (Which, by the way, I strongly recommend simply because it's easier. More white notes, if you get my drift...)

*H*owever, if you start playing in a group, you might find yourself with a guitar player who insists on playing the blues in F (which is very common in a group setting). If this ever happens, understand that the notes I've given you won't work. Instead you'll need the F blues scale (assuming you're playing in the key of F...). It is beyond the scope of this book to get into all of the different keys you could play in, so just suffice it to say that you'll need to get some more information should your playing lead you into a group setting.

What's the big secret? It's the fact that these six notes all sound equally as good whether you are in the C section, the F section, or the G section of the blues. No "clammy" sounding notes, nothing that will ever sound like a clunker. It makes for totally stress-free improvising while you're playing the blues. As long as you stick to those six notes, and nothing but those six notes, you will always sound great while you are making up a melody to play with your right hand.

This is one of those rare techniques that is at the same time very simple and yet extremely widely used by players everywhere. Guitar players in particular use the blues scale like crazy when they are soloing. After you practice getting these six notes really ingrained into your psyche, you will start hearing it used over and over in music you listen to on the radio or on recordings.

I strongly encourage you to work on getting the blues scale really comfortably "under hand." By that I mean get to the point where you can effortlessly move up or down a few octaves with your right hand smoothly playing up and/or down the blues scale.

Once you get comfortable playing the notes in the scale with your right hand, try to play the blues chords in your left hand (or maybe the voicings I gave you in one of the left hand examples) while you randomly play some notes in the scale with your right.

It will probably be a bit of a struggle at first trying to solve the coordination issue of getting your two hands to operate independently. Just fight your way through it and keep going slower and slower until you get to a tempo that allows you to play both hands.

You need to get to a point where you can play chords with your left hand and a random string of blues scale notes with your right hand. Once you do, it is as though you are standing at the edge of a steep cliff looking down into the seemingly mystical world of jazz improvisation. Honest to goodness, that's what improvisation is at its core: playing a melodic line conceived on-the-fly, made appropriate depending on what chords are clipping by in the tune.

Well, using the blues scale is TOTALLY appropriate for improvising a melodic line to the blues. It just happens to be made insanely simple because the same six-note scale works for all three chords you will come across in the blues chord progression.

Simple, appropriate, sounds great…just our style!

http://www.scottthepianoguy.com/book/examples/blues9.html

COMPING

Just to make you feel musically "in-the-know," the type of playing where you rhythmically play just the chords in a progression (in this case the twelve measure blues progression) is called "comping."

Comping is what piano players in jazz groups do most of the time when they are not either playing the melody or soloing themselves. It is the correct way to accompany someone else who is soloing.

To take it a step further, it is also the correct way to accompany *yourself*. Although that sounds a bit odd at first, when you think about it, a piano player has a little tougher row to hoe when it comes to improvising or soloing. First of all you need to play the melodic improvised line. At the same time you need to keep the chords going in some sort of accompaniment to your improvised line. Comping is the great answer to the accompaniment conundrum (say those last two words ten times quickly, whew...).

Comping in its basic form is really simple. You simply play the chord changes in some rhythmic pattern as they come down the line. This is opposed to simply playing a chord once and holding the chord down for the whole measure as you were doing earlier in the book.

The rhythm that you use is totally up to you. It can be a one or two measure rhythmic pattern repeated over and over. It can also be a totally random non-repeating pattern. You can make some of the chords very short and choppy (staccato for you musicians out there) and others you can hold down for a few beats. It is totally up to you.

For fear of sounding like a broken record, the best way to learn how to sound good using these techniques is to hear some piano players playing in real life and imitate the heck out of them. Find out where a jazz trio is playing and make a night of it (you look like you could stand to get out more any-way...). Try to get a spot where you can not only hear, but see the piano player. You'll get a huge dose of comping all night long.

Alternatively, go buy some recordings of jazz groups and start listening. Trios or quartets are great to listen to because not only does the piano player have to comp a lot all night, but you can hear it really well due to the relatively small group size. Now that you know what comping is, I think you will really be amazed how much time a piano player spends on it in a jazz or blues setting.

Since there are so many variations of comping, I'll give you a few different audio examples of comping at the addresses list-ed below:

http://www.scottthepianoguy.com/book/examples/comping1.html

http://www.scottthepianoguy.com/book/examples/comping2.html

http://www.scottthepianoguy.com/book/examples/comping3.html

CHAPTER 9

WHERE DO YOU GO FROM HERE? ANYWHERE YOU WANT!

It's about now in most books of this type that the author gives you a myriad of suggestions for further study materials, more exercises to follow up with, etc. As I pondered that next step when authoring this text, I realized that the very exercises I might suggest would be a lesson in futility for the vast majority of readers. Why? Because I don't have any clue as to what style of music you are interested in playing, or even more importantly, why you are interested in learning how to play in the first place! Until I know that, how pompous I would be to presume that I could give you solid suggestions as to what might come next in your piano playing life. Unless you happened to be a clone of me (Now that is a scary thought!) my directions would lead you to "Scott-ville" not "You-ville."

DRIVE THE TRAIN TO "YOU-VILLE"

YOU are the only one who can drive the train because YOU are the only one who knows what gets you excited (musically). One of the most mysterious, yet wonderful things about music is the fact that it appeals to everyone differently. What you like may or may not be what I like. Even more, what you like today may not be what you like tomorrow. (*Does anybody remember the Bay City Rollers? What in the heck was I thinking back then . . . yikes.*)

The point is this… Now that you have gotten the basics from this book, you have the base knowledge to go in ANY musical direction you want. As I have been describing in this whole book, it is *all* based on chords and reading lead sheets. So, for goodness sakes, you better make sure that the direction you're heading is one in which *you* are interested. Don't worry about me, some private teacher, your Mom or Dad, or your family – worry about YOU!

If you can't answer the question "What is the tune or style you have always wanted to play on a piano?" then stop right here and don't come back until you can. Until you know the answer to that question, you have no road map to tell you where to start your journey.

Once you *do* know the answer to that question, run, don't walk, to a music store or some on-line music retailer and get your hot little hands on that tune, or tunes in your favorite style. Believe it or not, that is what you should start with *first*.

That's right, gang. As unbelievable as it sounds, I'm telling you again to go get the tune you have always wanted to play more than anything else in the world, and make that the VERY FIRST TUNE in your soon to be expanding repertoire. Now I know many of you are still reverting to your trained Pavlovian response and throwing up mental roadblocks like: "That's too hard to start with…" or "I need to go practice for hours on end first."

Bzzzzt, incorrect, wrong-oh Mary Lou… Let's think about this for just a minute. I hope that by now you realize that this exercise of getting through a tune revolves around learning a few chords that are in whatever tune you are playing, right? Without question, you are going to have to learn a few chords. Well, why not learn the chords that are in the tune you have always wanted to play the most, first! Makes sense, doesn't it? I mean, why spend the next umpteen months of your life drilling through hundreds of chords and every varia-tion of them when you are only going to need a few to get through your most cherished tune of all time?

Why not just learn those few chords, stick them with the one note melody line, and start playing *your* tune tonight (or tomorrow, or maybe in a few days, but *certainly* not months or years down the road as traditional lessons would make you believe is necessary). You'll be having more fun than you've ever had in your life on a piano. Then, with all that pent up glee and enthusiasm you might just have an inkling to try the next tune down on your personal "hit parade" list. You learn whatever new chords you need *just to get through the tune you're working on* and start amazing your friends now with two great sounding tunes. (This is when people will start asking you who the heck your teacher is. Of course, you'll coolly respond that you don't have one, and that you're just kind of "picking it up as you go." If your guilty conscience gets the best of you, tell them where to go and buy this book. If not, your secret's safe with me…maybe…)

After you have repeated this episode a few times, you will magically find yourself transported to a place you probably thought you could never reach. That is where you can at any time, with no stress, sit down at a keyboard without music and just plain sound good performing some of your favorite tunes. You will also amaze yourself with the fact that you will have fairly effortlessly memorized quite a few chords by the time you have gotten through five or six tunes. Best of all, you did it without practicing at all. Instead you focused on playing a tune that you loved, then repeated that process over and over. By only spending your precious time working on having fun, you kept the motivation you need to keep going. Believe me, as an adult with probably a gazillion other things pressing in your life, it is the ONLY way you will probably ever get to this magical place. The minute this becomes work, you're doomed. As long as it stays fun, you're on the right track and not likely to get derailed.

A SPORTS ANALOGY

As an analogy, let's look at the sport of basketball. When it is all said and done, what is fun about playing basketball? Shooting a basket, right? Sure it is. Well, what if when we started kids playing basketball we told them that for the first year they were going to have to do nothing but dribbling and defensive drills? Then in the second year, they could only work on memorizing plays. Only after all of that will they be allowed to begin to start shooting at the hoop. How many kids do you think would make it through the first two years still interested in playing? Not many, that's for sure. Now I grant you that the ones that were bull-headed enough to stick it out would certainly have a quality, firm grasp of the fundamentals and would probably go on to become good players. The other 99%, however, would be forever cheated out of the opportunity to get the simple enjoyment of going out and shooting some baskets. Now if your goal was to become a professional basketball player, I could certainly see the wisdom in the years of working on fundamentals. But if you just wanted to have some fun, would it be such a crime to go shoot some baskets once in a while? Of course not!

Jump to our topic, playing piano, and you find much the same thing. You start taking classical lessons once a week. (By the way, more than likely, you were never even asked what type of music you were interested in playing. You just get started on Book 1 of whatever method your teacher uses just like all the rest of his/her students.) For months and months you work on scales, arpeggios, fingering, notation reading, and whatever else. After literally multiple years of work, you will finally get to a point where you are playing something enjoyable rather than another rendition of "Mary Had A Little Lamb" or some other beginning level tune.

Needless to say, the overwhelming majority of students

never get to this level of proficiency, and bail out. Too time consuming, too expensive, not enough fun, see ya later. Now the two or three percent that stick it out are certainly well rooted in the basics and fundamentals. They certainly have the background needed to possibly pursue a career as a classical pianist. (Those that don't get quite that lucky will probably end up teaching traditional piano at some point.)

The other 97% who quit, just like in the previous basketball example, are now going to be robbed of the opportunity to experience one of the most enjoyable things in the world – making music.

Why? Because as far as they're concerned, the piano lessons didn't work. These people never learned what I've talked about in this book. All their experience taught them is that playing piano equaled going and taking lessons once a week ad infinitum and so they failed. Again, if your goal was to become a professional classical concert pianist, I certainly see the wisdom in the years of working on fundamentals. But if you just want to have some fun making music, would it be such a crime to go learn some tunes using what I've just taught you? Of course not...

A PERSONAL PERSPECTIVE

On a personal note, there is nothing that I do in this world that gives me as much emotional satisfaction as simply sitting down and "playing a tune" at a piano. It's not about stress, not about perfection, not about incredible technique, or not about my "prodigal" talents (of which I have none...). It's about creativity. It's about letting whatever is in me at that exact moment in time come out my fingers and hopefully sound good. There's no one judging me. There's no one telling me whether it's "right or wrong." There's just me selfishly feeling good playing whatever in the world I want to play at that moment. Perfection and unbreakable rules are for balancing your checkbook, not playing piano.

Is there ego involved? Sure! Because not many people play, it is loads of fun when people ask you to sit down and play a tune…and you <u>can</u>. No stress, no needing to say no because "I don't have my music," no needing to make excuses for the lessons someone may know you have been taking for a while. You happily sit down and play something that sounds great and everyone has a ball and envies you. Yes, it can be good for your ego. But you know what? I'm still completely selfish about my playing.

SELFISH IS GOOD?

I realize that being selfish in our society is a trait that is to be avoided in almost all areas of your life, but in my opinion, this is where the exception lies. I am 100% selfish about my piano playing. I play only the tunes I like. I only play them in the style and at the speed in which I like to play them. When I'm tired of a tune I quit playing it. When I get bored with the tunes I'm playing, I learn new ones. If someone wants me to play a tune I don't like, I politely decline. Sounds logical, doesn't it? It is!

This is *your* project. It is *your* time and effort. It is *your* music. *You* play it the way you want to, be selfish, and refuse to play or work on anything that you don't like. I (or anyone else for that matter) can't tell you what tune to start with. Only you know what you like or are in the mood for at this moment. The minute something starts becoming drudgery, move on. Don't let the "it's too much work shark" catch you from behind. Just find a tune you like. Learn a few chords, play it (and maybe do a few cartwheels while yelling "I'm finally playing piano, YIPPEEEE!" at the top of your upside down lungs). Then move to the next "boy would I love to play (please insert your tune name here)" tune on your list. Tune after tune after tune…

METHOD, WHAT METHOD?

You see, I hate to sound like I'm tricking you, but there is actually a method to my madness. As I explained earlier, there are two different routes you can take to learn how to play non-classical piano. One way requires learning and memorizing hundreds of chords out of context (taking months and months to accomplish) and only then learning how to use them in tunes. The other way, which I feel is by far the superior way, is to learn chords through playing them in tunes. It's kind of like *on-the-job training*. I have proven to myself through the people I have taught in this style, that learning, memorizing, and getting new chords "under hand" is *greatly* simplified when you learn them in the context of a tune that you are excited about.

Educationally speaking, we know that an enjoyable, multi-sensory, hands-on approach to learning anything is far better than a rote, drill and practice approach! We need to apply this reality to piano playing. Have fun learning to play the piano and you too will be successful!

For example, how many times do you need to stick your finger into a flame to memorize that burning yourself is not a good idea? Once (I hope), because it involves many of your senses and emotions. Your touch tells you it's too hot, your nose decides that "char-grilled you" is pretty smelly, your eyes don't like the look of non-removable red on your fingertip, and most of all your emotions are screaming "ouch-ouch-ouch-pain-pain-pain-dumbthingtodo-dumbthingtodo-dumb-thingtodo!" That kind of an experience is pretty much burned into (sorry, I couldn't resist) long-term memory so deeply that you will never forget it – ever!

Now on the other end of the spectrum, let's picture cramming for some test you had in school. Most people can relate to having blindly memorized a bunch of facts for a test that you needed to take the next day. You could go in and regurgitate all of the info well enough to get a good grade on the test. Then a week or two later it was all gone…you couldn't take that test again and get nearly as good a score as you did the first time because you had forgotten so much of what you had memorized the weeks before. Why? Because you had nothing for your brain to "cement" the information to in your long-term memory. No practical use, no emotional attachment (positive or negative), nothing sensory-wise other than the memory of the visual image of the words you read. Remember, if you just memorize it, then spit it back out, you will lose it!

See the difference? That is why it is so vitally important to be selfish enough about your playing to never get caught playing something you don't enjoy emotionally. If it feels good, your brain is "cementing" it up in your noggin. If not, you are wasting precious time that keeps you from playing as much as you'd like to in the first place. After you learn chords in a tune you love playing, you've got 'em for life. They'll be there ready and willing to jump out of your fingers in some future tune that you may be playing whenever that particular chord symbol comes down the pike.

The "snowball" that is your knowledge of chords starts out small after you have learned your very first tune with the few chords that are in that tune. But boy does it start to pick up speed in a hurry and get bigger and bigger and bigger when you keep getting through new tunes.

You keep adding more and more new chords to the snowball, which makes each new tune simpler and simpler to play as you come across fewer and fewer new chords. It is a terrifically fun whirlwind to get caught in as your playing becomes better and better and simpler and simpler. It truly is having your cake and eating it too!

CHAPTER 10

IT'S TIME FOR THE LAST TUNE OF THE GIG...

If you have heard nothing else in this book, please hear this:

You <u>can</u> play piano!

Period.
End of story.

Assuming we are talking about non-classical styles of piano, you absolutely, positively have what it takes to play a tune at a piano. It just isn't that big an exercise.

It does not take some divine talent, some high degree of dexterity, long skinny fingers, superior intelligence, or whatever else you might have thought before now. What it also does not require is the ability to be a monstrously good notation reader. (Whether you knew it or not, that notation reading is what was, or what would have been, the real stumper for the vast, vast majority of you.)

What does it require? This...

1) You need to figure out how to identify the notes in the treble clef. (Remember Every Good Boy Does Fine and FACE?)
2) You need to figure out how to build chords, or easier yet, get a device that tells you what notes are in a particular chord.

3) You need to memorize whatever few chords are in the tune you are currently going crazy wanting to play.

4) You need to play the melody line with your right hand and the chords with your left hand.

Now that doesn't look like such rocket science, does it? It's not.

Is there a never-ending fountain of information that you can keep splashing in for as long as you want to improve? Absolutely, and I encourage you to get as wet as you want long after you have soaked up all that I have given you in this book.

Do you need to know all of that to get started, to sound good, and to have fun making music immediately? Absolutely not.

Remember, trust your ears, be selfish, and have fun!
Life's just too short to play dumb tunes… Go play piano.

EPILOGUE

I sure hope that you enjoyed reading the book. Even more so, I sure hope that you have started *playing*, not *practicing*, the piano.

I wanted to take these next couple of pages to let you know about the other things that I have going on in my quest to get the word out about how much fun playing piano can be for everyone!

WORKSHOPS AT EDUCATIONAL INSTITUTIONS

I give close to 100 workshops a year at universities and community colleges all over the country teaching this style of piano playing. The workshop is 3.5 hours long and is presented in one session, so it is very easy to attend from a scheduling standpoint.

I encourage you, if you would like to get some instruction from me in person, to consider attending a workshop. They are very fast paced, funny, and *very* motivational. If you think you need a little "kick in the pants" to get you going, I'm sure attending a workshop would do it.

Also, if I am not currently giving a class in your area, feel free to contact me with the name of a local university or community college that has a non-credit continuing education program. Alternatively, consider having me come to your area for a fund raiser or speech (see the next few pages for more info).

You can always find my schedule on my web site at:

http://www.scottthepianoguy.com

WORKSHOPS AS FUND RAISERS

Another venue in which I present my 3.5 hour piano workshop is for fund raisers for charitable organizations. It is exactly the same workshop that I present for educational institutions, but instead is hosted by an organization wishing to raise funds.

Basically, your organization simply finds a meeting space in which to hold the workshop, publicizes the date to the local media and its membership using provided press releases, and handles pre-registration. After the workshop, a significant portion of the per person registration fee goes directly to your organization.

Typical types of groups that have been interested include:

- Parent/Teacher Organizations
- Churches
- Social Sororities
- Junior Leagues
- Fraternal Organizations
- Band Booster Groups
- Hospital Foundations

If you are responsible for an organization's fund raising activities and would like some more information, please visit my web site at:

http://www.scotthouston.com

Once you get to the opening page, click on the button at the top that says "fund raisers." Also, please feel free to contact me at scott@scotthouston.com. We can send out a fund raiser kit with all of the details.

PUBLIC SPEAKING ENGAGEMENTS

In addition to giving piano workshops at educational institutions and fund raisers, I also do public speaking engagements on a variety of topics, all using music as a metaphor for real life situations.

A few of the topics include:

• Change Your Tune to Chase the Blues Away *(Motivational)*
• Create Your Own Orchestra *(Team Building)*
• Become Your Own Maestro *(Career Planning/Advancement)*
• Recording Your Own Financial Hit *(Financial Planning)*

Each speech is actually more of a "performance," through the use of multimedia musical equipment that is intertwined with the presentation. The combining of real life situations with the analogy of building a piece of music note-by-note, part-by-part, makes for an intriguing multi-sensory experience that audience members will remember for a lifetime. Each performance ends with all of the individual parts of music built and heard throughout the speech coming together to create a glorious, motivational, musical climax!

It truly turns a traditional keynote speech into an ***event!***

If you, or your company or organization, is interested in discussing my performing a speech at a company event, convention, or other function, feel free to email my office at scott@scotthouston.com.

HOME STUDY INSTRUCTIONAL MATERIALS

If you have been looking for more instructional materials on this type of piano playing, you might be a bit frustrated. This is because there is simply not much material (and even less that is of top quality information) out there in print that discusses this style of chord playing.

Although there are a few specialty sheet music stores around, in the majority of cases retail music stores focus on selling equipment, not sheet music or instructional books. They just don't make as much money on the "ink and paper" products. Therefore, in an effort to keep inventory costs as low as possible, they tend to stock what is requested by their customers. In the case of piano materials, their customers are overwhelmingly traditional classical piano teachers. Because very few teachers teach this style of playing, books on this topic just don't sell very well through traditional sheet music channels. Because they historically have not sold very well, publishers are not very thrilled about publishing music books on this topic. Whew, that was probably more than you wanted to know about the sheet music business. But now you know why it's tough to find good materials on this style of playing.

To solve this problem for the thousands of people who have taken my workshop, and now for those of you who have read this book, I offer a few select materials on my web site. The majority of the instructional materials on my site are not available in retail music or book stores. The exception to that are the fake books I offer from my site, which are available in the retail market. I offer those as a convenience to those of you who can't find any in your local music stores.

I assure you that I heartily endorse anything I have on my site. There is nothing I make available that I haven't seen or used in person. I also offer a no-questions-asked guarantee on anything sold from my site so there is no risk to you whatsoever. The site address is:

http://www.scottthepianoguy.com

APPENDIX

CHORD CHARTS

MAJOR CHORDS

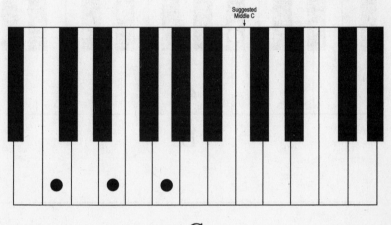

Suggested
Middle C

C

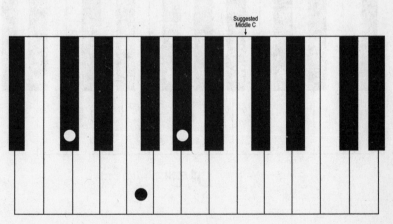

Suggested
Middle C

C#/D♭

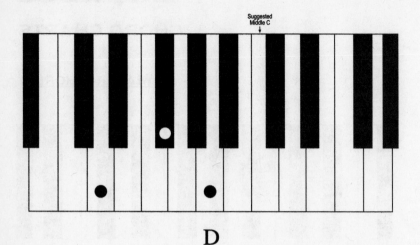

D

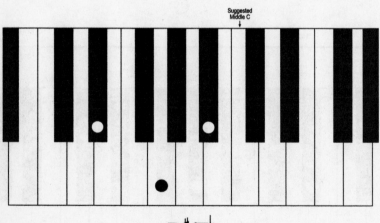

D♯/E♭

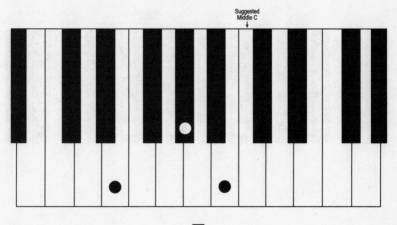

E

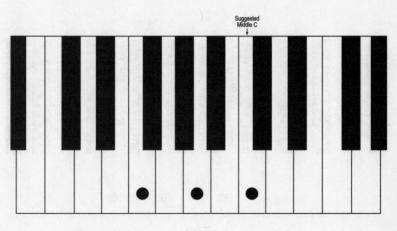

F

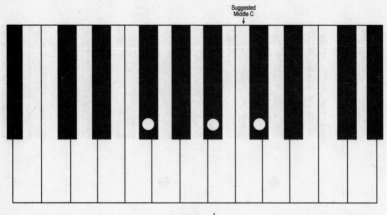

F#/G♭

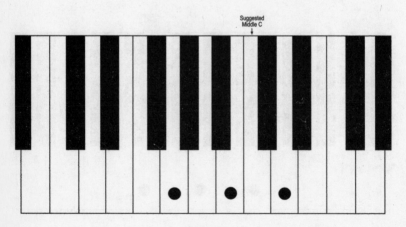

G

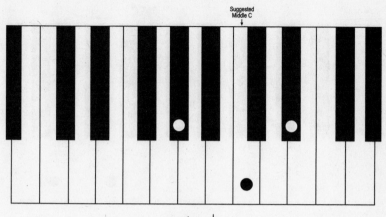

$G^{\#}/A^{\flat}$

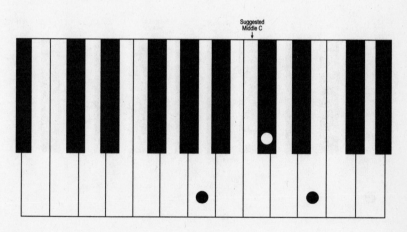

A

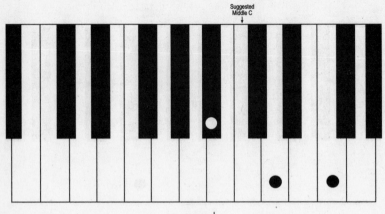

A#/B♭

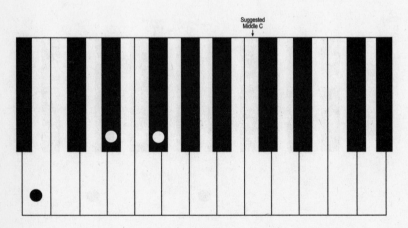

B

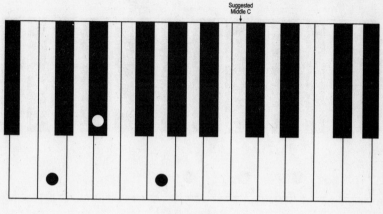

Cmin

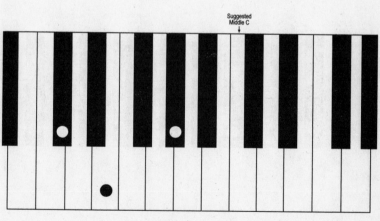

C#/D♭ min

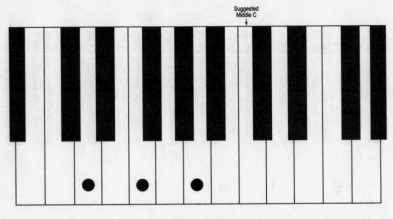

D min

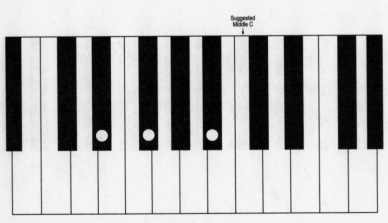

D[#]/E^b min

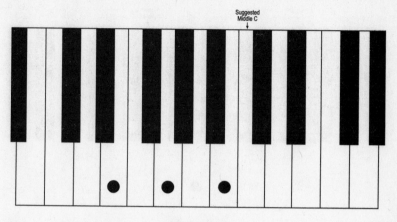

E min

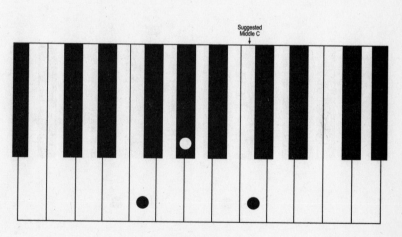

F min

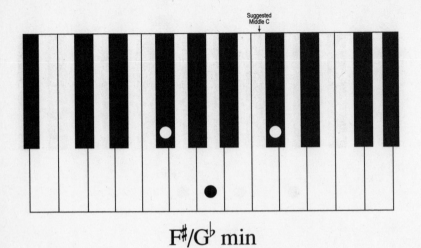

F#/G♭ min

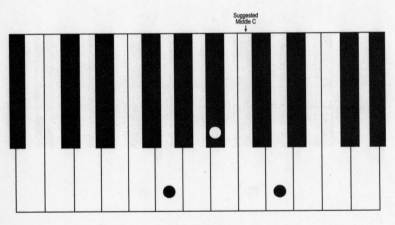

G min

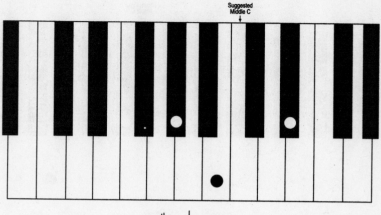

G#/A♭ min

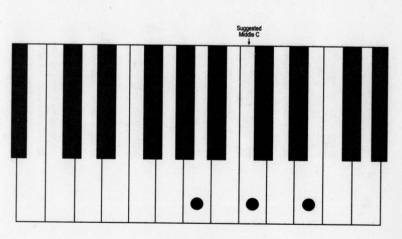

A min

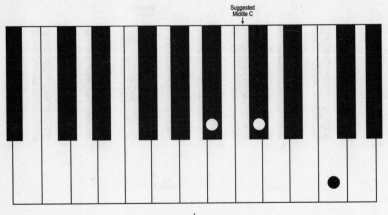

A$^\sharp$/B$^\flat$ min

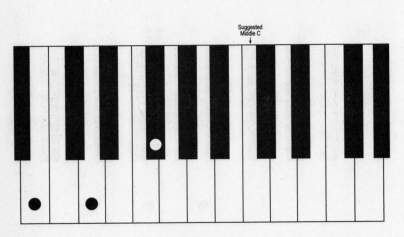

B min

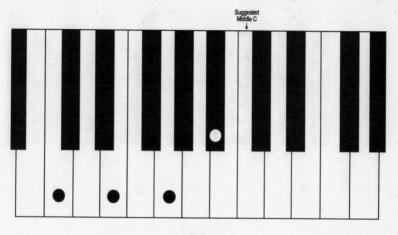

C7

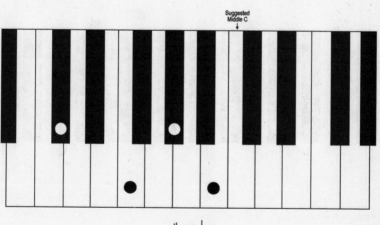

C#/D♭7

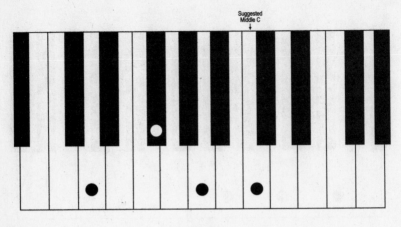

D7

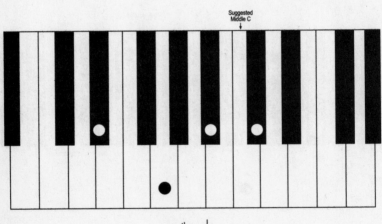

D#/E♭7

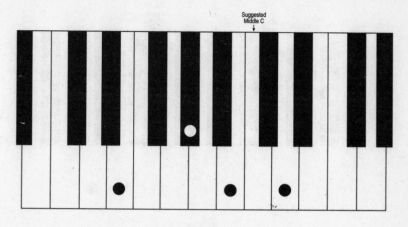

E7

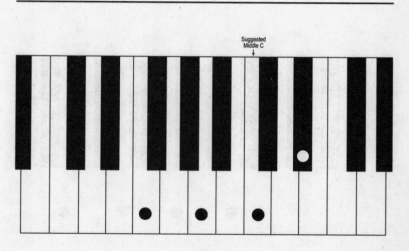

F7

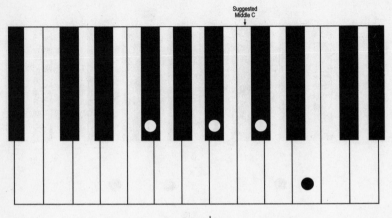

F#/G♭7

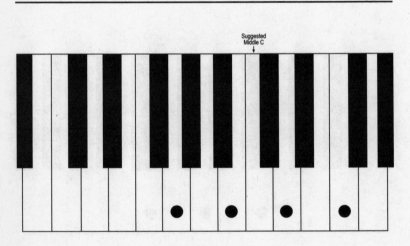

G7

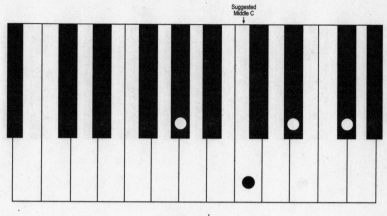

$G^{\sharp}/A^{\flat}7$

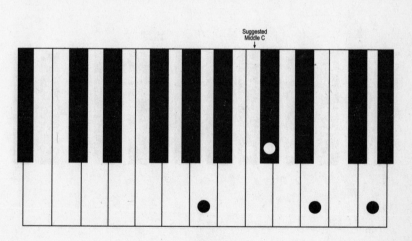

A7

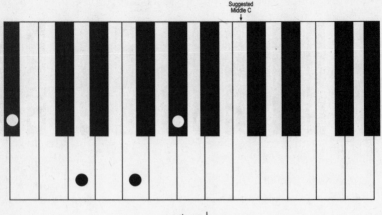

A♯/B♭7

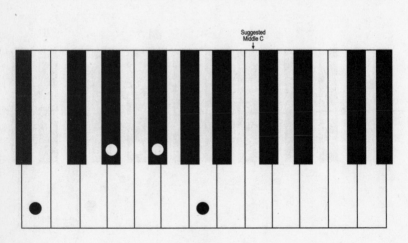

B7

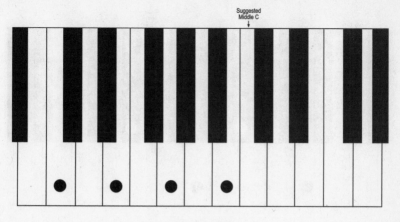

Cmaj7

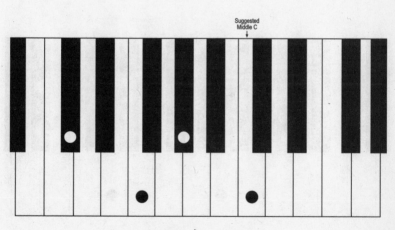

C#/D♭maj7

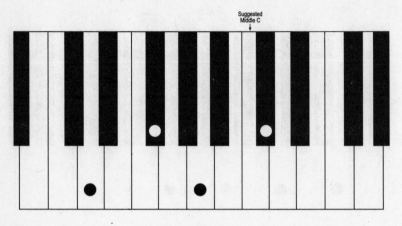

Dmaj7

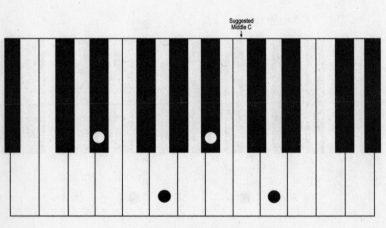

D#/E♭maj7

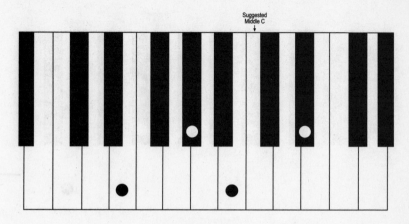

Emaj7

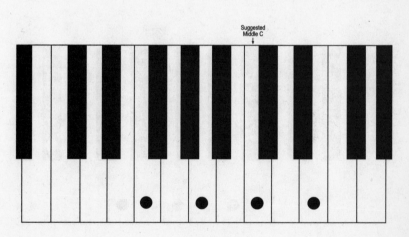

Fmaj7

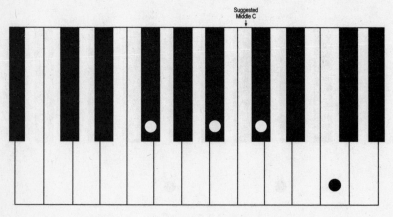

F#/G♭maj7

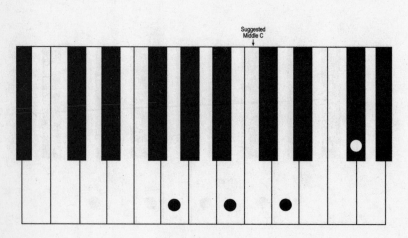

Gmaj7

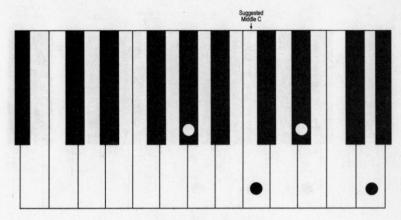

G#/A♭maj7

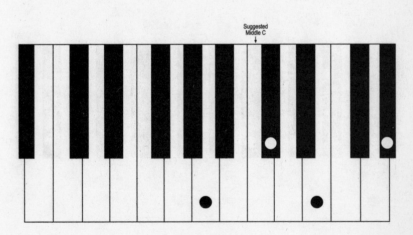

Amaj7

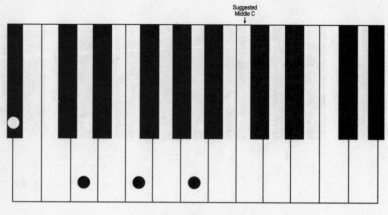

A#/B♭maj7

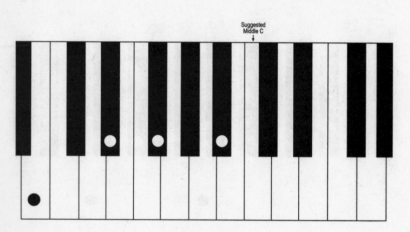

Bmaj7

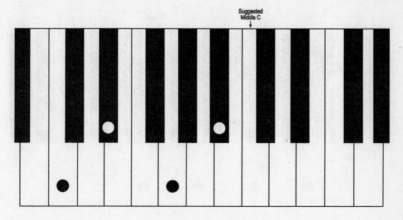

Cmin7

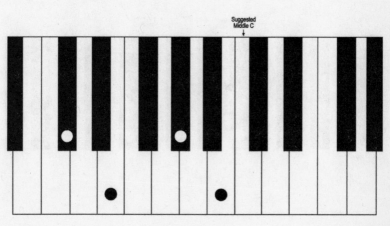

C#/D♭min7

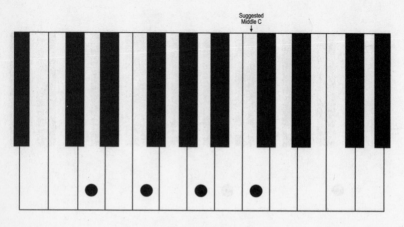

Dmin7

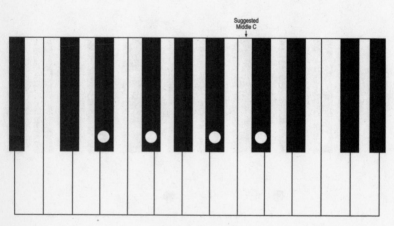

D#/E♭min7

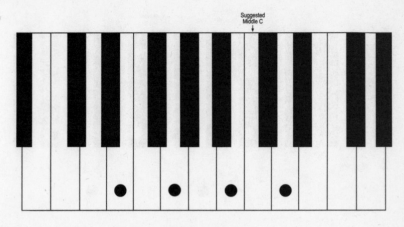

Emin7

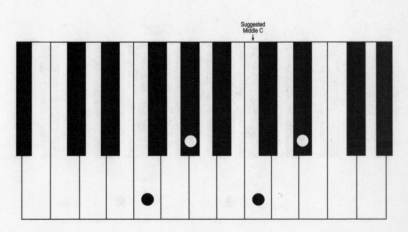

Fmin7

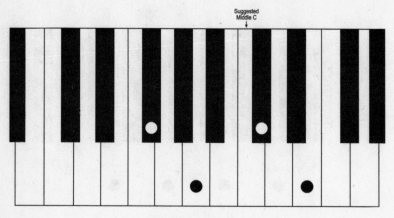

F#/G♭min7

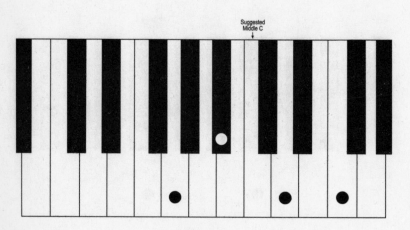

Gmin7

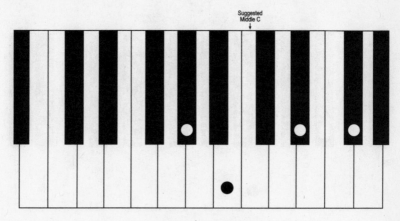

G#/A♭min7

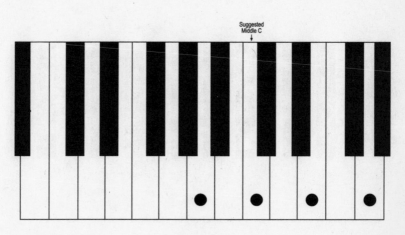

Amin7

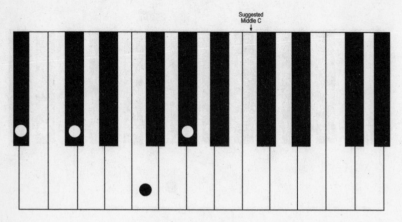

A#/B♭min7

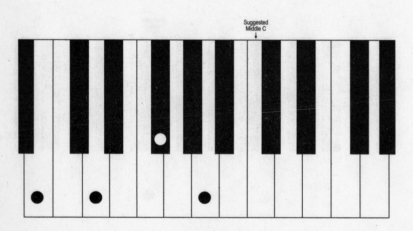

Bmin7

AUGMENTED CHORDS

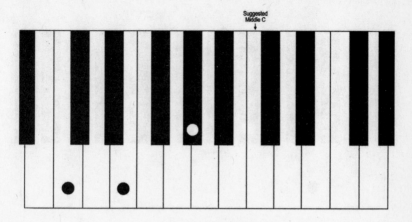

C aug

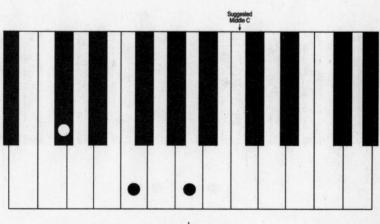

C#/D♭ aug

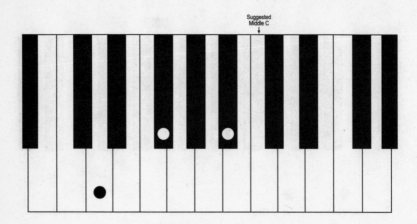

D aug

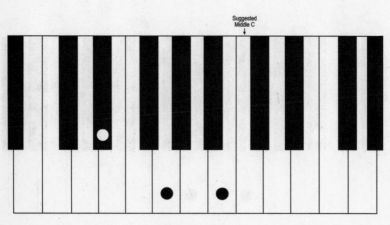

D#/Eb aug

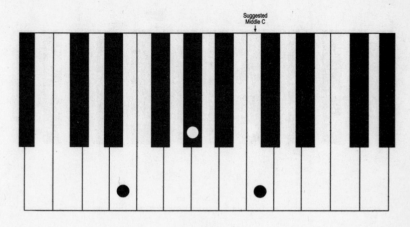

E aug

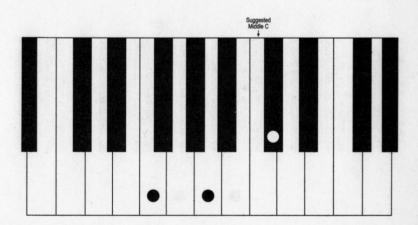

F aug

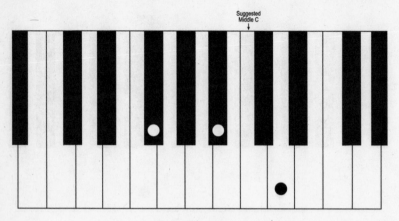

F#/G♭ aug

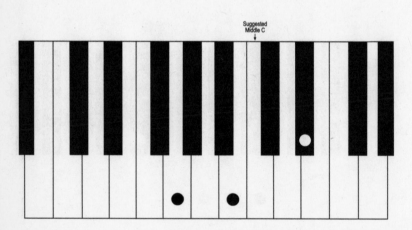

G aug

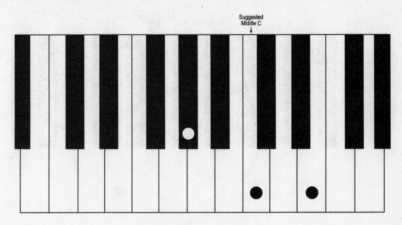

G#/A♭ aug

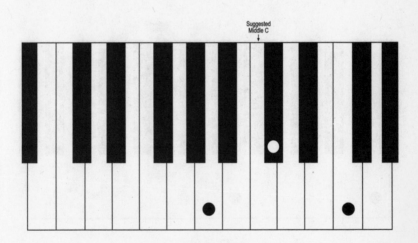

A aug

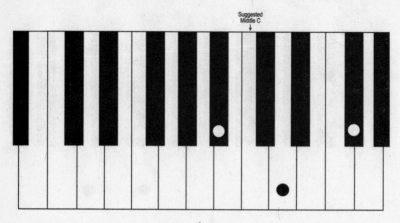

A#/B♭ aug

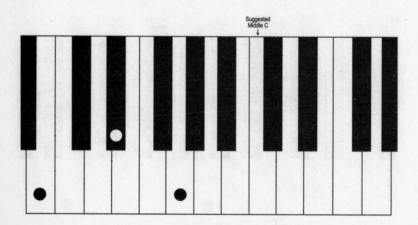

B aug

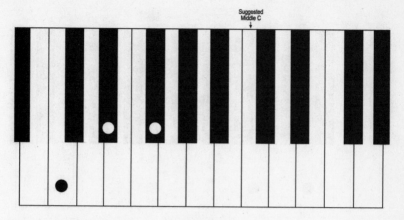

C dim

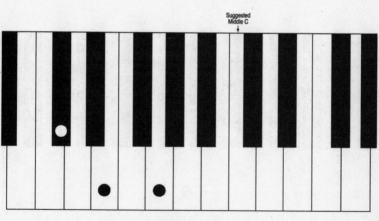

C#/D♭ dim

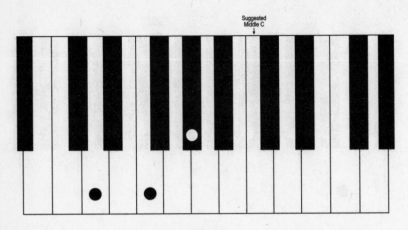

D dim

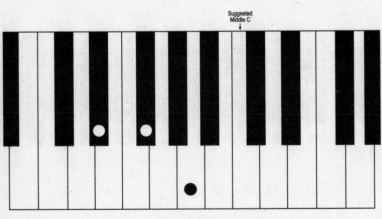

D#/E♭ dim

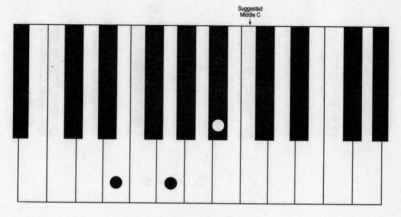

E dim

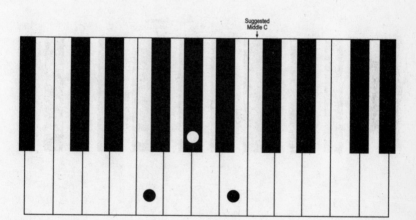

F dim

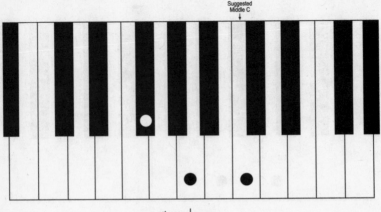

F#/G♭ dim

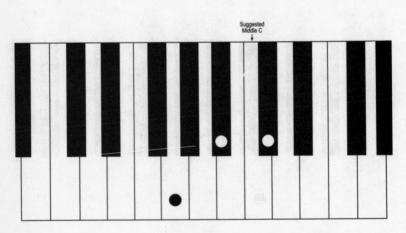

G dim

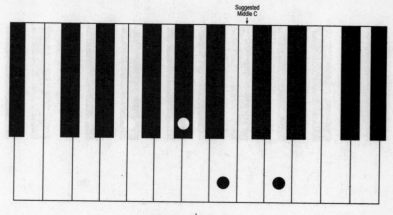

G♯/A♭ dim

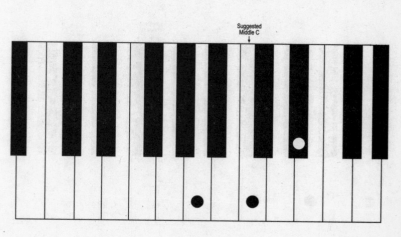

A dim

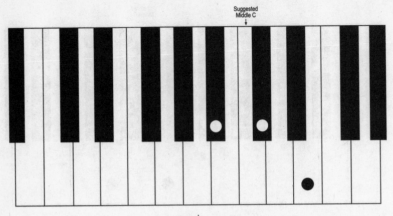

$A^{\sharp}/B^{\flat}$ dim

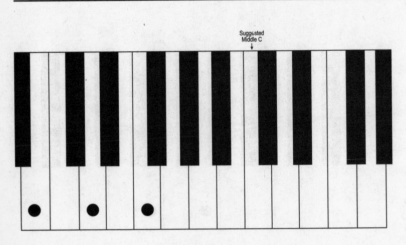

B dim